Ad Mashiach Nagid

The Messiah In Daniel 9

Ad Mashiach Nagid

The Messiah In Daniel 9

Robert M. Pill

First impression - January 2025
Published by Robert M. Pill
Ad Mashiach Nagid: The Messiah In Daniel 9
Copyright © 2025 by Robert M. Pill, All Rights Reserved.

For Jewish Scripture quotations:
Hebrew and English text for the Jewish Scriptures was taken from 'The Pill Tanakh: Hebrew-English Jewish Scriptures' copyright 2022-2024 by Robert M. Pill. Self–published as a three volume book: Volume 1 The Torah (the first five books of Moses — Genesis – Deuteronomy), Volume 2 The Prophets (Joshua – Malachi), and Volume 3 The Writings (1 Chronicles – Nehemiah). The order of the books in The Pill Tanakh is the exact same order as found in the ancient Leningrad Codex, also known as The Masoretic Text!

Book Typesetting, and Cover Design by Robert M. Pill
Cover image is from a "scratch" Watercolor painting by the author around 1982.

ISBN: 979-8-9882917-3-2 (Soft Cover)
ISBN: 979-8-9882917-4-9 (eBook)

First Edition: Year: 2025 Month:

12 11 10 9 8 7 6 5 4 3 2 **1**

כִּי תִּמָּלֵא הָאָרֶץ כִּי יד ב
לָדַעַת אֶת־כְּבוֹד יְהוָה
כַּמַּיִם יְכַסּוּ עַל־יָם:

2 14 For the earth shall be filled with the knowledge of the glory of Yehovah, as the waters cover the sea.

[Habakkuk 2:14 The Pill Tanakh]

Table of Contents

Introduction 1
Daniel 9:25 9
Ad Mashiach Nagid 25
Gabriel Knew! 47
Biblical Judaism 55
The Ten Commandments 67
Seek Yehovah 79
Epilogue 95

Introduction

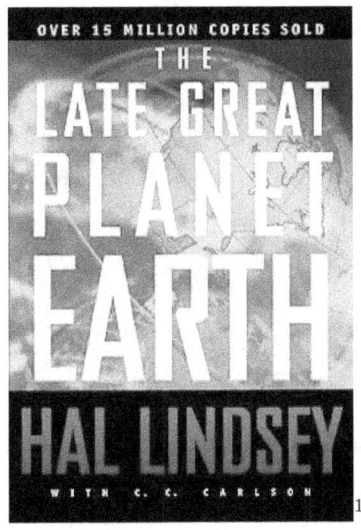

The book, 'The Late Great Planet Earth,'[2] was a huge influence on American society after its release in 1970.[3]   Similar views have also been propagated from the influence of other Christian writings, including Messianic Jewish writers like Dr. Arnold Fruchtenbaum![4]

Many people came to learn about prophetic, Biblical, passages, such as found in **Daniel 9:25,** which have been interpreted to be

[1]Hal Lindsey with C.C. Carlson, "The Late Great Planet Earth," (Grand Rapids, MI, Zondervan).

[2]Long before the Left Behind books crowded the New York Times best-seller list, Hal Lindsey and C. C. Carlson's The Late Great Planet Earth introduced millions of readers worldwide to end-times prophecy. An accessible, engaging introduction to the coming apocalypse, The Late Great Planet Earth was the best-selling nonfiction book of the 1970s: Ten million copies were in circulation by the end of the decade. It sold more than 28 million copies by 1990, an estimated 35 million by 1999, and was translated into more than 50 languages.
Erin A. Smith, 'The Late Great Planet Earth Made the Apocalypse a Popular Concern', HUMANITIES. Winter 2017.   Volume 38.   Number 1, accessed 23 Oct 2024, https://www.neh.gov/humanities/2017/winter/feature/the-late-great-planet-earth-made-the-apocalypse-popular-concern

[3]My own atheist mother bought the book around that time. After she read it, she asked me and my brother to read it. Thus, although we were non-religious and also atheists, we were informed about the Christian 'premillennial/dispensational' prophetic belief system!

[4]Arnold.Fruchtenbaum, Ariel Ministries - Bible Teaching From A Messianic Jewish Perspective, 'Dr. Fruchtenbaum', accessed 10 Oct. 2024, https://www.ariel.org/about/dr-fruchtenbaum.

about the coming of **the person** known as **The Messiah,** and specifically to **Jesus.** It is often translated to say that **he would be cut off,** i.e. die; and many Christians believe that it is a prophecy which forecasts *that Jesus would be crucified* .

Thus, many came to believe and understand that, in the first century time frame, there was no other prominent figure who might have been considered to be **The Messiah** other than the man, **Jesus of Nazareth.**

ט כה וְתֵדַע וְתַשְׂכֵּל מִן־מֹצָא דָבָר
לְהָשִׁיב וְלִבְנוֹת יְרוּשָׁלַם עַד־מָשִׁיחַ נָגִיד
שָׁבֻעִים שִׁבְעָה וְשָׁבֻעִים שִׁשִּׁים וּשְׁנַיִם
תָּשׁוּב וְנִבְנְתָה רְחוֹב וְחָרוּץ וּבְצוֹק
הָעִתִּים:

9 25 Know therefore and discern, that from the going forth of the word to return to and to build Yerushalam unto Mashiach Nagid shall be seven weeks; and for sixty-two weeks, it shall be built again, with broad place and moat, but in troublous times.
[Daniel 9:25 The Pill Tanakh]

It is known from recorded history that **the seven weeks** (49 years) **to the building of Yerushalam**[5] was fulfilled (Daniel 9:25). Cyrus is understood to have given the 'דבר ~ Devar (word)' to return to and build Yerushalam at around the year **538.**[6]

---

[5]I refer to the **holy city** as Yerushalam in my self–published three volume book, 'The Pill Tanakh: Hebrew–English Jewish Scriptures.' I do not do this casually — it is intentional! In the Hebrew–language based Jewish Scriptures, 'Yerushalam' is the simple transliteration (in English it is typically rendered as 'Jerusalem'). 'Yerushalam' is simply my transliteration of the Hebrew יְרוּשָׁלַם. Of note is that I provide the transliteration of יְרוּשְׁלֶם 'Yerush'lem' as it occurs in Aramaic portions of Daniel and Ezra. Also, the extremely rare transliteration of יְרוּשָׁלַיִם 'Yerushalyim' occurs in only four places in the entire Jewish Scriptures (Jeremiah 26:18, Esther 2:6, 1 Chronicles 3:5, 2 Chronicles 25:1)!

[6]These principles find expression in the Hebrew edict issued to the Jews of Babylonia (538 B.C.E.), which appears in Ezra 1:2–4 (see also II Chron. 36:23). There Cyrus attributes his decision to erect the temple to a command of God, just as he attributed his actions in Babylon

From popular books like 'The Late Great Planet Earth,' and those from other authors, the expectation was promulgated that the Messiah would have come at *the end of 62nd week* (62 x 7 = 434 years, Daniel 9:25b).

Nevertheless, by looking at the date of "the word" from Cyrus, *if* it **was around the 538 BCE,** then 49 years later (7 weeks / 7 sevens) would have brought us to around the date of **489 BCE** when returning to and building **Yerushalam** would have begun. **If we then subtract 434 years (62 x 7),** that would bring us to about the year **55 BCE. Obviously, that time frame predates Jesus!**

However, there are several other, later dates,[7] **which some expositors consider to be when the *'word'* was given to return to and build Yerushalam.** Those dates work better to interpret Daniel's timeline to coincide with Jesus, as well as some tying the destruction of Yerushalam's 2nd Temple at the time of Roman conquest in 70 C.E.

Recently, after much contemplation, rereading the Daniel passages many times in Hebrew and English, and praying for understanding, I have now come to view these passages in a different way!

---

to an order of Marduk. An additional document of his concerning the erection of the Temple is more administrative in nature and deals with the architectural and financial details of building (Ezra 6:3–5); this document is even written in Aramaic, the administrative language. As a result of the permission given by Cyrus, some of the Babylonian exiles returned to Judah, and with their return a new chapter in the history of Israel began – the period of the Second Temple.
The Jewish Virtual Library, `Cyrus (559-529)', accessed 14 Oct 2024, https://www.jewishvirtuallibrary.org/cyrus.
    [7]**Four Persian Decrees**
1. **538/7 BC:** Cyrus allowed Jews to return to Judah and to rebuild the temple (Ezra 1:1-4; cf. Isa 45:1).
2. **About 520 BC:** Darius I reaffirmed and expedited the order of Cyrus (Ezra 6:1-12).
3. **457 BC:** Artaxerxes I granted a decree to Ezra (Ezra 7:12-26) to re-establish the autonomy of Judah.
4. **445/444 BC:** Artaxerxes I permitted Nehemiah to repair Jerusalem.
Andries Van Niekerk, 'From Daniel to Revelation', accessed 23 Oct 2024, https://revelationbyjesuschrist.com/decree-to-restore-jerusalem/

I must step back and give a caveat having to do with the angel Gabriel's declaration *that the understanding of the visions are for a later time,* found in Daniel 8:26, 12:9:

ח **כו** וּמַרְאֵה הָעֶרֶב וְהַבֹּקֶר אֲשֶׁר נֶאֱמַר אֱמֶת הוּא וְאַתָּה סְתֹם הֶחָזוֹן כִּי לְיָמִים רַבִּים:

8 **26** And the vision of the evenings and mornings which hath been told is true; but thou, shut thou up the vision; for it belongeth to many days to come.' [Daniel 8:26 The Pill Tanakh]

יב **ט** וַיֹּאמֶר לֵךְ דָּנִיֵּאל כִּי־סְתֻמִים וַחֲתֻמִים הַדְּבָרִים עַד־עֵת קֵץ:

12 **9** And he said: 'Go thy way, Daniel; for the words are shut up and sealed till the time of the end. [Daniel 12:9 The Pill Tanakh]

I bring this up because **there are many voices expressing that they <u>absolutely</u> <u>know</u> how the end–times' prophecies are to be fulfilled.** Most people who speak to this have a Christian, premillennial, dispensational world view, like Hal Lindsey and Dr. Arnold Fruchtenbaum. Their reasoning is based, mostly, upon prophecies in the books of Daniel and Ezekiel in the Jewish Scriptures, and the writings of Paul and the book of The Revelation in the Christian Scriptures, aka the New Testament.

However, most who hold that view rely upon a *juxtaposition of the Hebrew text in Daniel 9:25* and a modified timeline that requires changing the times to fit their narratives, **i.e. to make the prophecies work and to support their belief system.** Moreover, to add to this **interpretation confusion,** English translations may have contributed to a fundamental misunderstanding of the Hebrew text![8]

---

[8]see my analysis of לְהָשִׁיב L'hashiv in the chapter titled **'Ad Mashiach Nagid.'**

In my opinion, many of these people are sincere, but they are so consumed with their narrative that they cannot objectively examine the ancient Biblical passages in their natural contexts.

I have come to the position that interpreting the Hebrew–language based Jewish Scriptures away from their natural contexts is very dangerous. I have said elsewhere that I think it is a breach of the 9th commandment in the same sense as lying, bearing a false witness against others.

Is it possible that those who hold to this practice are knowing deceivers? Or, is it possible that these folks do not know Biblical Hebrew and are just ill–informed?

If that is the case, any knowledge of Biblical Hebrew would likely depend upon a *'questionable'* understanding of others they may deem as experts!

Or, is it the result of the fact, as the angel Gabriel stated several times, **that these things are sealed up until the time of the end?** No doubt but that also must come into consideration!

There are three passages in the Jewish Scriptures which speak to the idea that **you should not add to or take away from the 'Word of G–d'** (Deuteronomy 4:2, 13:1, Proverbs 30:6). That idea is also expressed in last book of the Christian New Testament, the Revelation to John (Revelation 22:18–19).

I am quite aware that those admonitions apply to me as well!

However, I can and do read the Hebrew and try to discern and interpret, based upon my own understanding. When I read the Hebrew and come across words or phrases I am unsure about, I want to look them up in Hebrew-English Dictionaries to help give me a better understanding.[9]

---

[9]My 'go–to' dictionaries are:
Ernest Klein, 'A Comprehensive Etymological Dictionary of the Hebrew Language for Readers of English', Sefaria, accessed 9 Mar 2021, https://www.sefaria.org/Klein_Dictionary.
Reuben Alcalay, ''The Complete English Hebrew Dictionary,'' (Tel Aviv–Jerusalem, Massadah Publishing).

I recognize that I can be wrong, as I have certainly held different views in the past, but now see that my interpretations were greatly influenced by others and I was not able to see things as I do now.

I consider that the Leningrad Codex, also known as the Masoretic text, is the authoritative Hebrew–language based Jewish Scriptures. [10] When I self–published my three volume Tanakh,[11] 'The Pill Tanakh: Hebrew–English Jewish Scriptures,' **I put the books of the Jewish Scriptures in the same order that the Masoretes placed them,** which is different from most, if not all, Jewish and Christian Bibles.[12]

---

[10]"Let us say on the outset that the Leningrad Codex is one of the most important Hebrew documents extant, with ramifications and influence that is immeasurable. It is - along with the other famous biblical codex, the Aleppo Codex - one of the sources for biblical tradition, for the study of Hebrew Scriptures, and for providing an accurate text for the reading and writing of the Torah and the other books of the Bible."
Curt Leviant, "Jewish Holy Scriptures: The Leningrad Codex," Jewish Virtual Library, accessed 19 May 2022, https://www.jewishvirtuallibrary.org/the-leningrad-codex.

[11]Tanakh. "Though the word "Bible" is commonly used by non-Jews -- as are the terms "Old Testament" and "New Testament" — the appropriate term to use for the Hebrew scriptures ("scripture" is a synonym used by both Jews and non-Jews) is Tanakh. This word is derived from the Hebrew letters of its three components:
Torah: The Books of Genesis (Bereshit), Exodus (Shemot), Leviticus (Vayikrah), Numbers (Bamidbar) and Deuteronomy (Devarim).
Nevi'im (Prophets): The Books of Joshua, Judges, I Samuel, II Samuel, I Kings, II Kings, Isaiah, Jeremiah, Ezekiel, Hosea, Joel, Amos, Obadiah, Jonah, Micah, Nahum, Habukkuk, Zephaniah, Haggai, Zechariah, and Malachi. (The last twelve are sometimes grouped together as "Trei Asar" ["Twelve"].)
Ketuvim (Writings): The Books of Psalms, Proverbs, Job, Song of Songs, Ruth, Lamentations, Ecclesiastes, Esther, Daniel (although not all that is included in the Christian Canon), Ezra and Nehemiah, I Chronicles, and II Chronicles."
Shamash Hadash, "The Tanakh," Jewish Virtual Library, accessed 25 April 2021, https://www.jewishvirtuallibrary.org/the-tanakh.

[12]In Jewish Publications the order of books is most noticeable in the section known as 'Writings;' but in the 'Prophets' Samuel and Kings are complete units, whereas in both Christian Bibles and also in 'The Pill Tanakh' they have been separated into two parts, such as 1 & 2 Samuel, 1 & 2 Kings.
In the writings section, most Bibles place Chronicles as the last book(s) (Jewish Bibles have just one book for Chronicles, Ezra and Nehemiah, whereas other renderings have them broken up into 1 & 2 Chronicles and separate books for Ezra and Nehemiah). In The Leningrad Codex, as well as in The Pill Tanakh, 1 & 2 Chronicles appear at the beginning of 'The Writings' section. Also, in The Pill Tanakh, Ezra and Nehemiah are separate books at the end.
The order of the books of the 'Writings' section, as they appear in the Leningrad Codex and The Pill Tanakh are as follows: 1 & 2 Chronicles, Psalms, Job, Proverbs, Ruth, Song of Songs, Ecclesiastes, Lamentations, Esther, Daniel, Ezra, Nehemiah.

In the writing of my version of the Jewish Scriptures, I sourced my Hebrew text from the Westminster Leningrad Codex,[13] the digitized form of which I had used my copyrighted C++ Library to write C++ code to convert from a Multi–wide UTF–16 Unicode format (not editable) to my copyrighted ASCII based UTF–8 web–font format (editable).

My base English text is from the Jewish Publication Society version of 1917 (JPS1917).[14]

For both Hebrew and English texts, I altered the Hebrew and English to actually conform to the verse separations of the Leningrad Codex for the Ten Commandments (Exodus 20, Deuteronomy 5)!

I believe it to be noteworthy that other Jewish and Christian Biblical publications all break up both the Hebrew and English texts for **The Ten Commandments** *differently than the Masoretic Text, aka The Leningrad Codex!*

I made other changes to conform to the actual Hebrew of The Leningrad Codex, and to the translation of the English text as I found appropriate to correspond to the Hebrew text.[15]

---

[13] J. Alan Groves Center For Advanced Biblical Research, ''Westminster Leningrad Codex,'' accessed 27 May 2022, https://www.grovescenter.org/projects/westminster-leningrad-codex/.

[14] Mechon Mamre, ''The Hebrew Bible in English according to the JPS 1917 Edition © 2002 all rights reserved to Mechon Mamre for this HTML version,'' accessed 17 Jan 2015, https://mechon-mamre.org/e/et/et0.htm

[15] For the catalog of changes I made to both Hebrew and English texts in my online Tanakh (https://www.the-iconoclast.org/resources/tanakh/tanakh.php) and my self–published Hebrew–English Tanakh, see https://www.the-iconoclast.org/images/changes_copyrighted_material.pdf.

Daniel 9:25

Two Opposing Interpretations of Daniel 9

1) A Jewish Interpretation by Rabbi Bentzion Kravitz

The book of Daniel is filled with Messianic illusions and calculations that even left Daniel pondering their meanings. Additionally, a large proportion of the book is written in Aramaic rather than the traditional Hebrew adding to the complexity of these biblical texts.

The ninth chapter has been of interest to both Jews and Christians.

The message of a merciful God communicated in verse 18, "for not because of our righteousness do we pour out supplications before You, but because of Your great compassion." has been a foundation of a Jews personal and spiritual relationship with God.

Christians on the other hand tend to focus of verses 24 - 26. The following is the Christian translation of those verses:

24) Seventy weeks are determined upon your people and upon your holy city, to finish the transgression, and to make an end of sins, and to make reconciliation for iniquity, and to bring in everlasting righteousness, and to seal up the vision and prophecy, and to anoint the most Holy.

25) Know therefore and discern that from the issuing of a decree to restore and rebuild Jerusalem until Messiah the Prince will be seven weeks and sixty-two weeks; it will be built again with plaza and moat but in troubled times.

26) Then after sixty-two weeks the Messiah will be cut off but not for himself and the people of the prince who is to come will destroy the city and the sanctuary."

Many Christians assert that these passages are a prophecy that predicts the exact dates that the Messiah will come and also die. They believe that Jesus fulfilled these predictions.

...

UNDERSTANDING DANIEL

Now we can return to the beginning of Daniel 9 and establish the correct starting point for Daniel's prophesy.

The Christian major error in establishing the starting point of Daniel's prophecy is caused by their mistranslation of the verse, "Know therefore and discern that from the going forth of the decree to restore and rebuild Jerusalem." Daniel 9:25

Since their translation asserts that the starting point of this prophesy is from the issuing of a certain decree to rebuild Jerusalem, they incorrectly assume that it is the decree of King Artaxerxex. However, as mentioned above, there were several different decrees made concerning returning and rebuilding Jerusalem.

In Daniel 9:25 the original Hebrew used the word (דבר ~ Devar) which is significantly different from a human decree. The word (דבר ~ Devar) refers to a prophetic word. In the beginning of Daniel 9 verse 2, this word is used when Daniel says that he wants to understand "the word of the Lord to the Prophet Jeremiah."

As mentioned above, in all the passages that mention some form of decree or proclamation concerning Jerusalem, none of them use the Hebrew word (דבר ~ Devar).

The correct translation of Daniel should be:

"Know therefore and discern that from the going forth of the word to restore and rebuild Jerusalem." Daniel 9:25

Therefore, the correct starting point of Daniel's prophesy must be associated with the issuing of a prophetic word and not a human decree.

...

This is how Daniel 9:24-26 should be correctly translated and understood:

24) Seventy weeks (490 years) are determined upon your people and upon your holy city, to <u>finish</u> the transgression, and to make an end of sins, and to make reconciliation for iniquity, and to bring in everlasting righteousness, and to seal up the vision and prophecy, and to <u>anoint the Holy of Holies</u>.

25) Know therefore and discern that from the issuing of <u>a word</u> to restore and rebuild Jerusalem (starting from its destruction) until <u>an anointed Prince</u> (Cyrus) will be <u>seven weeks</u> (49 years) <u>and then for sixty-two weeks</u> (434 years) it will be built again with plaza and moat but in troubled times. (Persian, Greek, and Roman domination)

26) Then <u>after the sixty-two weeks</u> (483 years from the destruction of the First Temple) an <u>anointed one</u> (sacrifices, last Jewish priest and king) will be cut off <u>and will be no more</u>, and the people of the prince (Romans) who is to come will destroy the city and

the sanctuary. (in the 70th week 490 years from the destruction of the First Temple)

This is a brief explanation of Daniel chapter 9. Any attempt to apply this chapter to Jesus is erroneous and wrought with mistranslations and misinterpretations.[1]

2) A Messianic Jewish (Christian) Interpretation by Dr. Arnold Fruchtembaum

...

The 70 sevens are divided into three separate units—seven sevens, 62 sevens and one seven. During the first time period (49 years) Jerusalem would be "built again, with street and moat, even in troublous times." The second block of time (62 sevens, a total of 434 years) immediately followed the first for a total of 69 sevens, or 483 years.

It is at this point that we are told what the ending point is of the 69 sevens: "unto Messiah the Prince." As clearly as Daniel could have stated it, he taught that 483 years after the decree to rebuild Jerusalem had been issued, Messiah would be here on earth.

The obvious conclusion is this: If Messiah was not on earth 483 years after a decree was issued to rebuild Jerusalem, then Daniel was a false prophet and his book has no business being in the Hebrew Scriptures. But if Daniel was correct and his prophecy was fulfilled, then who was the Messiah of whom he spoke?

...

[1]Rabbi Bentzion Kravitz, 'Daniel 9 – A True Biblical Interpretation', Jews For Judaism, accessed 2 Oct 2024, https://jewsforjudaism.org/knowledge/articles/daniel-9-a-true-biblical-interpretation/

Conclusions

This dramatic prophecy features certain things in very clear and unmistakable terms. First, the Messiah was to be on earth 483 years after the decree to rebuild Jerusalem. Secondly, after his appearance on earth he was to be killed, not for his own sins, but rather for those of others; and the death he would die was to be the death of the penalty of the law. Thirdly, the death of the Messiah had to come sometime before Jerusalem and the temple were destroyed again, which occurred in the year 70 C. E. Fourthly, some time after the destruction of Jerusalem and the temple, and following a long period of warfare, the 70th seven will commence, and once that has run its course, Messiah's kingdom and age of righteousness will be established. For that to occur, the implication is that the Messiah who was killed would return again.

But who is this Messiah? One man fulfills all that is required in this passage. Jesus of Nazareth was born into the Jewish world and proclaimed his messiahship 483 years after the decree to rebuild and restore Jerusalem was issued. In the year 30 C. E., Jesus was executed by crucifixion. Daniel indicated that he would be cut off, not for himself, but rather for others. Isaiah 53 also prophesied the death of the Messiah, pointing out that he would die a substitutionary death on behalf of his people Israel. The teaching of the New Covenant is that Jesus died a penal death by taking upon himself the penalty of the Law as a substitute for his people. In keeping with Daniel 9:24, he died for the purpose of making an atonement for sins. Three days after his death, he was resurrected. Finally, the New Covenant proclaims the fact that he will someday return to set up his kingdom and the age of righteousness.

If Daniel was right, then Messiah came and died prior to the year 70 C.E. If Daniel was right, then there are no other options for who the Messiah is, but Jesus of Nazareth. If Daniel was right, this Jesus is destined to return and to set up the messianic kingdom.[2]

Two Distinct Sections in Daniel 9:25

Silluq and Ethnacta (Cantillation Marks)[3]

There are a three primary cantillation (trop) marks in the Masoretic Hebrew text which are important in knowing logical breaks in longer verses and where each verse terminates.

In the ancient, handwritten Leningrad Codex, Masoretes marked a verse's end with a cantillation mark which is called **Sof-Pasuq** (סוֹף פָּסוּק:), that looks like a colon (:). The **Sof-Pasuq** cantillation mark designates the end most verses, **_but not all verses!_**

Another cantillation mark, called **Silluq** (סִילוּק), a small vertical line to the left of the vowel mark having the word's primary accent, **is found in the last word of each and every verse in the entire Tanakh –** the Jewish Scriptures written in the ancient **Hebrew Leningrad Codex!**

הָעִתִּים: is in the last word of Daniel 9:25 (the **Silluq** is found under the Tav – תֵ, to the left of the **Hiriq** vowel (dot under the Hebrew letter). Note that there is also a **Sof–Pasuq** at the end of the word.

---

[2]Arnold G. Fruchtenbaum, 'Daniel 9 – The Coming Of The Messiah', One For Israel, accessed 25 Sep 2024, https://www.oneforisrael.org/uncategorized/daniel-9-the-coming-of-the-messiah/. (notation given of Copyright © 2009 Jews for Jesus)

[3]Joshua R. Jacobson, ''Chanting the Hebrew Bible: The Complete Guide to the Art of Cantillation'' (Philadelphia, PA, The Jewish Publication Society), pp 32-47.

The **Silluq** is called an **Emperor Accent.** <u>There</u> <u>are</u> <u>only</u> <u>two</u> <u>Emperor</u> <u>Accents</u> (cantillation marks – trop) in the ancient Masoretic text.

The second **Emperor Accent** is called **Ethnacta** (אֶתְנַחְתָּא – an Aramaic word). It typically appears in longer verses. As with the **Silluq,** this cantillation mark appears to the left of a word's primary accent mark. <u>**The Ethnacta marks the end of the first part of a verse,**</u> **and the Silluq marks the end of the second part of longer verses.**   The **Ethnacta** is shaped like an upside down 'u' or 'v' with a vertical tick mark at its top [˄].

In Daniel 9:25, there is an **Ethnacta** appearing in שָׁבְעִים שִׁבְעָה (seven weeks), which designates the end of the first part of the verse. There is a **Silluq and a Sof–Pasuq at the end of the second part, designating the end of the verse.**

The first part of Daniel 9:25, ending with the **Ethnacta** cantillation mark, is as follows:

טכה   וְתֵדַ֣ע וְתַשְׂכֵּ֗ל מִן־מֹצָ֣א דָבָר֮ לְהָשִׁיב֒
וְלִבְנ֣וֹת יְרוּשָׁלִַ֗ם עַד־מָשִׁ֣יחַ נָגִ֔יד שָׁבֻעִ֖ים שִׁבְעָ֑ה

9 **25** Know therefore and discern, that from the going forth of the word to return to and build Yerushalam unto Mashiach Nagid shall be seven weeks; [Daniel 9:25a]

This is a complete and independent expression of thought!

The appearance of the **Ethnacta** makes it clear that the Masoretes believed the verse is to be **separated into two parts,** again ending the first part of the verse with שָׁבְעִים שִׁבְעָה (seven weeks / seven sevens).

The second part of Daniel 9:25 is

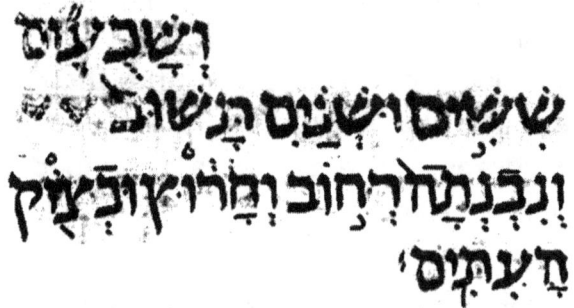

וְשָׁבֻעִים שִׁשִּׁים וּשְׁנַיִם תָּשׁוּב וְנִבְנְתָה רְחוֹב וְחָרוּץ וּבְצוֹק הָעִתִּים:

and for sixty-two weeks, it shall be built again, with broad place and moat, but in troublous times. [Daniel 9:25b]

I would like to note that the first part of the verse not only ends with the cantillation mark, **Ethnacta,** but the **first word of the second part of the verse** begins with the letter vav [וְ], which is typically understood to mean **'and.'**

That first phrase of the second portion of the verse begins with וְשָׁבֻעִים שִׁשִּׁים וּשְׁנַיִם, interpreted to say '*and* *for sixty–two.*'

If you were not willing to recognize the **Ethnacta** as ending the first part of the verse, the word וְשָׁבֻעִים beginning with [וְ] and translated as **'and'** certainly presents an argument which clearly designates the start of the second part of the verse!

Both of the above interpretations by Rabbi Bentzion Kravitz and Dr. Arnold Fruchtenbaum want to make the entire verse say something different than what the actual Hebrew says!

However, I believe that Rabbi Bentzion Kravitz's commentary is closer to the correct interpretation of the Hebrew. Yet, in my opinion, *his **parenthetical remarks*** do not reflect actual Scriptural references. ***Could it be that they are from the rabbinical collection of books known as the Talmud?*** [4] In my opinion, when those ***parenthetical remarks*** are presented within the interpretation, they force a different meaning to the actual Hebrew text!

Most Christian interpretations want to connect the idea of ***The Messiah*** with the second part of the verse, rather than in the first part, where the Hebrew grammar naturally places it. **That is a juxtaposition of the Hebrew text,** and employing a translation in that way definitely takes the Hebrew out of its plain and simple meaning and its natural context.

---

[4] *Talmud* (literally, "study") is the generic term for the documents that comment and expand upon the Mishnah ("repeating"), the first work of rabbinic law, published around the year 200 CE by Rabbi Judah the Prince in the land of Israel.
About the Talmud
Although Talmud is largely about law, it should not be confused with either codes of law or with a commentary on the legal sections of the Torah. Due to its spare and laconic style, the Talmud is studied, not read. The difficulty of the intergenerational text has necessitated and fostered the development of an institutional and communal structure that supported the learning of Talmud and the establishment of special schools where each generation is apprenticed into its study by the previous generation.
The Mishnah
In the second century, Rabbi Judah the Patriarch published the Mishnah in six primary sections, or orders, dealing with agriculture, sacred times, women and personal status, damages, holy things, and purity laws. By carefully laying out different opinions concerning Jewish law, the Mishnah presents itself more as a case book of law. While the Mishnah preserved the teachings of earlier rabbis, it also shows the signs of a unified editing. Part of that editing process included selecting materials; many of the traditions that did not "make it" into the Mishnah were collected in a companion volume called the Tosefta (appendix, or supplement).
MY JEWISH LEARNING, 'What Is the Talmud? — *An intergenerational rabbinic conversation that is studied, not read.*', accessed 18 Nov 2024,
https://www.myjewishlearning.com/article/talmud-101/

In my opinion, both groups want to interpret ancient Jewish Scriptures in a context of modern understanding, and apply to it their embellished expositions to *prove* their points.

Dr. Arnold Fruchtenbaum's statement on Daniel 9:25b:

> It is at this point that we are told what the ending point is of the 69 sevens: "unto Messiah the Prince." As clearly as Daniel could have stated it, he taught that 483 years after the decree to rebuild Jerusalem had been issued, Messiah would be here on earth.

Just like most dispensationalists/premillennialists, Dr. Arnold Fruchtenbaum associates the 2nd part of verse 25 with **The Messiah.** He **misinterprets** the simple and plain meaning of the Hebrew context in which he interprets the coming of **The Messiah** to appear at the end of the 69th week of the prophecy!

He also made this following statement in his article:

> **The obvious conclusion is this: If Messiah was not on earth 483 years after a decree was issued to rebuild Jerusalem, then Daniel was a false prophet and his book has no business being in the Hebrew Scriptures.**

My concern with that statement is that Dr. Fruchtenbaum may be putting himself in the position of being a *false prophet!* **He makes a claim that if the interpretation is not fulfilled *according to his view*,** then he states, "... Daniel was a false prophet ...."

Unfortunately, for Dr. Fruchtenbaum, *it is his own interpretation that is false,* because he does not interpret the Hebrew text properly, but rather takes it out of the plain and simple meaning of its natural context **without any regard to the Hebrew grammar!**

He juxtaposes verse 25, associating עַד־מָשִׁיחַ נָגִיד (unto Mashiach Nagid) **with the second part of the verse.** However, as I showed above, that phrase naturally belongs in the first part of the verse. I believe that is clearly a very poor exegesis. In the least, it is a flawed representation of the Hebrew of the Masoretic Text!

Rabbi Bentzion Kravitz on Daniel 9:25:

> 25) Know therefore and discern that from the issuing of a word to restore and rebuild Jerusalem (starting from its destruction) until an anointed Prince (Cyrus) will be seven weeks (49 years) and then for sixty-two weeks (434 years) it will be built again with plaza and moat but in troubled times. (Persian, Greek, and Roman domination)

Rabbi Bentzion Kravitz associates the 'word to restore and build Jerusalem' from the original destruction of Jerusalem by Nebuchadnezzar, but he considers Cyrus as an anointed prince (עַד־מָשִׁיחַ נָגִיד – unto Mashiach Nagid) as prophesied by Isaiah. He dates it *not* from 'the word to restore and build Jerusalem,' but rather from the original destruction of the Temple in Jerusalem. Thus, he associates the beginning of Daniel's discourse from verses 1 and 2 as if it is a continuation of Gabriel's words *appearing later in the chapter!*

However, he properly represents the last part of verse 25 correctly, as it is separated by the *Ethnacta* at (שָׁבְעִים שִׁבְעָה) seven sevens (49 years) and then begins the 62 weeks part of the prophecy!

Rabbi Kravitz ends his argument with the following statement:

This is a brief explanation of Daniel chapter 9. Any attempt to apply this chapter to Jesus is erroneous and wrought with mistranslations and misinterpretations.

A Couple of Key Take Aways
From Those Two Opposing Viewpoints

1) To reiterate, the Hebrew text of Daniel 9:25 is split apart into two distinct parts. The cantillation mark, **Ethnacta,** designating the end of the first part of the verse, is found at the end of the words for seven weeks (שָׁבְעִים שִׁבְעָה).

There is absolutely no doubt that עַד־מָשִׁיחַ נָגִיד 'Ad Mashiach Nagid' is associated with the first part of the verse — the seven weeks (שָׁבְעִים שִׁבְעָה) — forty-nine years from the time of *the word* to return to and build Yerushalam.

Thankfully, the Masoretes added these cantillation marks in addition to the vowel pointers. **Thus, we not only know how to pronounce the words but we also know how to break the verses apart into their logical sections and to end them.**

2) Rabbi Kravitz wants to start the time to numbering the 49 years (seven weeks) from the destruction of the Temple in Jerusalem by Nebuchadnezzar. It appears to me that he wants to do so, basing his timing in lieu of Daniel questioning when Jeremiah's prophecy of when Yehovah[5] would accomplish for the desolations of Yerushalam seventy years (Daniel 9:2). He no doubt interprets this based upon his understanding of דבר ~ Devar, which to him is "a prophetic word."

I do not believe that the angel Gabriel's words in Daniel 9:25 support that interpretation. The text simply states that from the time of the word to return to and build Yerushalam עַד־מָשִׁיחַ נָגִיד **"unto Mashiach Nagid"** (Daniel 9:25) would be seven weeks.

---

[5]If interested in knowing more about The Name יְהֹוָה — Yehovah, I refer you to the excellent resources by Dr. Nehemia Gordon found at his website: https://www.nehemiaswall.com/nehemia-gordon-name-god, or a teaching in a YouTube video which may be found at https://www.youtube.com/watch?v=YfljMUR9dKA.

It is also noteworthy that Rabbi Kravitz associates **Cyrus with being the Mashiach Nagid,** but it seems doing so is not so much as saying Cyrus is there, at that time, but that perhaps to show that the prophecy is somehow fulfilled in that way.

Moreover, at the beginning of the book of **Ezra,** Ezra clearly shows the time of the fulfillment of 'the word' to return to and build Yerushalam!

אֵ א וּבִשְׁנַת אַחַת לְכֹ֫ורֶשׁ מֶ֫לֶךְ פָּרַס לִכְלֹות
דְּבַר־יְהֹוָה מִפִּי יִרְמְיָה הָעִיר יְהֹוָה אֶת־ר֫וּחַ
כֹּ֫רֶשׁ מֶ֫לֶךְ־פָּרַס וַיַּעֲבֶר־קֹול֙ בְּכָל־מַלְכוּתֹו
וְגַם־בְּמִכְתָּב לֵאמֹֽר:

1 1 Now in the first year of Cyrus king of Persia, that the word of Yehovah by the mouth of Jeremiah might be accomplished, Yehovah stirred up the spirit of Cyrus king of Persia, that he made a proclamation throughout all his kingdom, and put it also in writing, saying:

בֵ כֹּה אָמַר כֹּ֫רֶשׁ מֶ֫לֶךְ פָּרַס כֹּל מַמְלְכֹות
הָאָ֫רֶץ נָתַן לִי יְהֹוָה אֱלֹהֵי הַשָּׁמָ֫יִם וְהוּא־פָקַד
עָלַי לִבְנֹות־לֹו בַ֫יִת בִּירוּשָׁלַ֫ם אֲשֶׁר בִּיהוּדָֽה:

2 'Thus saith Cyrus king of Persia: All the kingdoms of the earth hath Yehovah, the God of heaven, given me; and He hath charged me to build Him a house in Yerushalam, which is in Judah. [Ezra 1:1–2 The Pill Tanakh]

Obviously, one of the stumbling blocks to understanding this prophecy could be discovering that both building Yerushalam

and also the Machiach Nagid occur in the same '49 year' time frame, as they are presented together in the first part of the verse (ending with the *Ethnacta* cantillation mark).

If, as dispensationalist/premillennialist Christians like Dr. Arnold Fruchtenbaum and Hal Lindsey who want to associate the term, עַד־מָשִׁיחַ נָגִיד (unto Mashiach Nagid), to Jesus, **it is quite obvious** that **Jesus did not come at the time of returning to and building Yerushalam,** forty–nine (49) years after the 'דבר ~ Devar (word)' was given (perhaps around the year **489 BCE**)!

According to Christian *apologetics*, Jesus came on the scene over four-hundred (400) years later! That certainly presents a conundrum **if they want to say that they are correctly interpreting the Hebrew text and honoring 'the word of God.'**

If Rabbi Kravitz is incorrect in his timing for the **forty-nine (49) years to date from the destruction of the Temple,** then associating Cyrus as Mashiach Nagid may also be questionable.

If anyone considers that "The Word of God is True," in my opinion, they must acquiesce to the simple and plain meaning of the Hebrew text and not misconstrue it to say something that it absolutely does not say!

All of us must be careful not to add to or take away from what we consider to be 'the word of the Almighty God!'

Unfortunately, forcing the text to say something that it clearly does not say may be a bit amateurish, but also may be deceptive! Moreover, it is quite possible that is a direct breaking of the 9th commandment.

Summary

In this chapter, I have tried to present how some of the modern views of end–time–prophecy have come about. I've provided a couple of opposing views from a more orthodox Jewish perspective and a Messianic Jewish (Christian) perspective.

I've examined the important text of Daniel 9:25, used as a basis for prophetic views, and analyzed them from looking at the actual Hebrew text. I've shown that by the placing of cantillation marks in the ancient text of the Leningrad Codex, by Masoretes, why the verse **must** be separated at the *Ethnacta* appearing in שָׁבְעִים שִׁבְעָה (seven weeks).

Additional Thoughts

Did the angel Gabriel know that his message to Daniel would be interpreted in many ways? Could that be one of the reasons he stressed that the vision was for a much later time?

If so, then could he have already foreseen that his message would be construed so that it would even bring about the new religion of Christianity?

What about עַד־מָשִׁיחַ נָגִיד **Ad Mashiach Nagid?** If both of the above views by Rabbi Kravitz and Dr. Fruchtenbaum are wrong, then still if Daniel was a true prophet, עַד־מָשִׁיחַ נָגִיד **Ad Mashiach Nagid** had to come into the picture of history at the time of the word to return to and build Yerushalam!

עַד מָשִׁיחַ נָגִיד
Ad Mashiach Nagid

I have purposefully titled this chapter, **'Ad Mashiach Nagid.'** My intention is certainly to provide definitions and analysis of key Hebrew words from Daniel 9:25, including עַד־מָשִׁיחַ נָגִיד **'Ad Mashiach Nagid,'** which make a difference in the understanding of this critical text.

Unfortunately, not everyone who tries to explain these verses in Daniel 9 have a good understanding of the ancient handwritten Hebrew found in *The Leningrad Codex*, aka the Masoretic text. Some actually choose to explain this verse using English translations without examining the actual Hebrew source!

L'hashiv — לְהָשִׁיב

One example is simply from the Hebrew word, לְהָשִׁיב **'L'hashiv,'** which is translated *'restore'* by many Bibles, including the JPS 1917!

The following Hebrew words are concordance–like definitions of the English word, **'restore'** to its Hebrew equivalent words as found in the Shiloh Hebrew–English Dictionary[1]:

הֶחֱיָה: שִׁקֵם קוֹמֵם: הֶחֱזִיר לְיָשְׁנוּ

In an effort to try and make it very clear what these Hebrew words mean, I am including their definitions, from their roots, as presented in The Shiloh Hebrew–English Dictionary:[2]

---

[1]Zevi Scharfstein and Rose Scharfstein, "Shiloh Dictionary Hebrew–English," Shiloh Publishing House, Publication Date 1933-05-05, © Copyright by Zevi Scharfstein.
Zevi Scharfstein and Rose Scharfstein, "Shiloh Dictionary Hebrew–English," accessed 29 Oct 2024, https://archive.org/details/hebrew-english-shiloh-dictionary/
[2]ibid.

הֶחֱיָה

חיה (חַי, חָיָה, יִחְיֶה) to

live; to exist; to survive, to revive

חִיָּה— to maintain; to

support; to revive; to heal

חַיָּה living being: animal; game; soul; sustenance, food

קוֹמֵם

קום (קָם, יָקוּם) to exist;

to arise; to stand; to stand up; to rise against; to be realized; to exist

קוֹמֵם— to raise

לִישְׁנוּ

שנה (שָׁנָה, יִשְׁנֶה) to repeat;

to be different; to study

הִשָּׁנֶה— to be repeated

שִׁנָּה— to alter, change;

to repeat; to remove

הִשְׁתַּנָּה— to alter, change;

to be changed; to disguise oneself

שִׁנָּה טַעְמוֹ— to change one's demeanor

שִׁקֵּם

שקה (שָׁקָה) to be

moistened, irrigated

הַשְׁקָה— to give to drink;

to water (cattle); to water, irrigate

שָׁקוּד industrious

שִׁקּוּי ז. drink; refreshment

שִׁקְמָה נ. (ר. שִׁקְמִים, שִׁקְמוֹת) sycamore-tree

הֶחֱזִיר

חזר (חָזַר יַחֲזֹר) to turn

back; to return; to repeat; to follow after; to repent

חִזֵּר— to walk about; to follow after

הֶחֱזִיר— to turn round; to return; to restore

חֲזָרָה נ. giving back;

repetition; turning back

בַּחֲזָרָה— back

Do any of those Hebrew words, which represent the English term **RESTORE**, appear in the text of Daniel 9:25? No! Absolutely not. So, we really need to look at the Hebrew word in the text and see if it should be translated differently!

"TO RETURN" – L'hashiv – לְהָשִׁיב

The following is the definition of the root of the word לְהָשִׁיב which is שׁוּב. The definitions are from Ernest Klein's' A Comprehensive Etymological Dictionary of the Hebrew Language for Readers of English.[3]

שִׁיבָה f.n. PBH coming back. [Verbal n. of שׁוּב. See שׁוּב and first suff. ־ָה.]

שָׁב adj. **1** one who returns. PBH **2** one who repents, penitent. [From שׁוּב [I].

שׁוּב [I] to return, turn back, come again, go again.
— **Qal** – **1** שָׁב he returned, turned back, came again, went again; **2** he became again; **3** he did again, repeated; MH **4** he became; **5** he repented (in this sense it is used elliptically for שָׁב מִדַּרְכּוֹ הָרָעָה, 'he returned from his evil way', or for שָׁב אֶל ה', 'he returned to the Lord'); **5** he changed his mind.
— **Pol.** – **1** שׁוֹבֵב he brought back, took back; **2** he restored, refreshed.
— **Po.** – שׁוֹבַב was brought back, was taken back, was restored.
— **Hiph.** – **1** הֵשִׁיב he caused to return, brought back; **2** he gave back, restored; **3** he answered, replied (in this sense used elliptically for הֵשִׁיב דָּבָר, lit.: 'returned word'); **4** he reversed,

[3]Ernest Klein, 'A Comprehensive Etymological Dictionary of the Hebrew Language for Readers of English', (CARTA, Jerusalem), Copyright © 1987 by The Beatrice & Arthur Minden Foundation & The University of Haifa.
Ernest Klein, 'A Comprehensive Etymological Dictionary of the Hebrew Language for Readers of English', Sefaria, accessed 9 Mar 2021, https://www.sefaria.org/Klein_Dictionary.

revoked.

— **Hoph.** — הוּשַׁב was returned, brought back, was restored. [Aram. (also BAram.) תּוּב (= to return, turn back, come again, go again), Syr. תָּב (= he returned, turned back, came again, went again), Ugar. tb (= to turn; to answer, comply with), Arab. thāba (= he returned, turned back, came back, went back), OSArab. תוב (= to return; to reward).] Derivatives: מוּשָׁב, מָשׁוֹב, מְשׁוֹבֵב, תְּשׁוּבָה, תִּיוּבְתָּא,.. cp. שׁוֹבֵב, שׁוּבָה, שִׁיב, שִׁיוּב, הֲשָׁבָה, הֶשָׁבוֹן.

In the definition for שׁוּב (Shin-Vav-Vet — Shuv), above, for both Hebrew grammar abbreviations **Hiph.** (Hiph'îl) [הֵשִׁיב] and **Hoph.** (Hoph'âl) [הוּשַׁב], which are both close to the spelling of לְהָשִׁיב — L'hashiv, the definitions express the idea of 'he caused to return, brought back' and 'was returned, brought back, restored.' Although the **Hoph.** (Hoph'âl) definition includes 'restored,' that still follows the sense of the main meaning, **which is 'to return!'**

As part of an internet search regarding **"restore and build Jerusalem,"** I happened upon at least one website that focused on parsing the English word **"restore!"** [4] That and similar posts add confusion, in my opinion, to this topic. Rather than looking at the Hebrew word used in the passage that is often translated "restore," they have gone off on illogical tangents to try to explain the text based upon the English translation itself!

In my opinion, לְהָשִׁיב L'hashiv should be translated as **'to return'** — **and not** 'to restore'!

עַד־מָשִׁיחַ נָגִיד

Ad Mashiach Nagid

---

[4]Andries Van Niekerk, 'Which decree began the 490 years of Daniel 9,' accessed 28 Oct 2024, https://revelationbyjesuschrist.com/decree-to-restore-jerusalem/

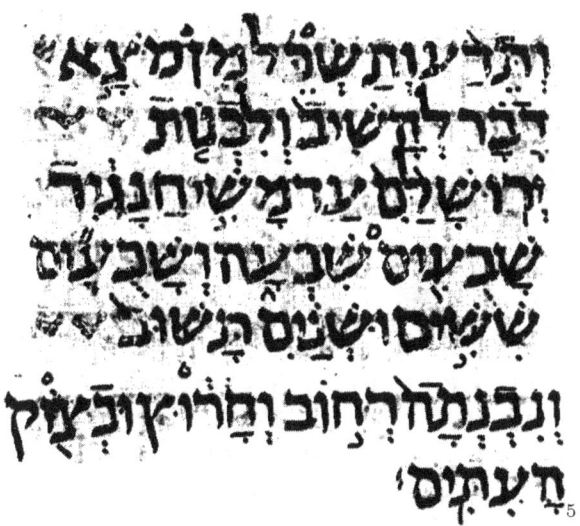

וְתֵדַע וְתַשְׂכֵּל מִן־מֹצָא דָבָר לְהָשִׁיב֙ **כה** **ט**
וְלִבְנוֹת יְרוּשָׁלַ֙ם עַד־מָשִׁיחַ נָגִיד שָׁבֻעִים שִׁבְעָה
וְשָׁבֻעִים שִׁשִּׁים וּשְׁנַ֔יִם תָּשׁוּב֙ וְנִבְנְתָה֙ רְחוֹב
וְחָר֔וּץ וּבְצ֖וֹק הָעִתִּֽים׃

9 25 Know therefore and discern, that from the going forth of the word to ***return*** to and build Yerushalam unto *Mashiach nagid* shall be seven weeks; and for sixty-two weeks, it shall be built again, with broad place and moat, but in troublous times.

[Daniel 9:25 The Pill Tanakh]

---

[5] The Leningrad Codex is the oldest extant Hebrew Masoretic manuscript of the entire Old Testament. The manuscript claims to have been written by Samuel ben Jacob in Cairo in 1008 and based on manuscripts by Aaron ben Moses ben Asher. It has been used as the basis for many printed editions of the Hebrew Bible.
INTERNET ARCHIVE, 'The Leningrad Codex (Codex Leningradensis)', accessed 15 Oct 2024, https://archive.org/details/Leningrad_Codex
Image from pdf file of Daniel 9:25 in The Leningrad Codex, grayscale applied, top of second column (end of verse) added to bottom of first column.

Ad Mashiach Nagid — Defined! [6]

עַד – Ad

עַד [I] prep. & conj. 1 to, unto, up to, even to. 2 until, while. [Older form עֲדֵי Derivatives: הָעֲנָנָה [II], הֶעֱנַנְוּת [II], עֵגֶן מַעֲנָן, מְעַנָּן m.n. NH anchor. [From Talmudic הוֹגִין, עוֹגִין , which is prob. borrowed from Gk. onkinos (ħook), from onkos (of s.m.), which stands in gradational relationship to Gk. ankos (ā bend, hollow), ankon (ƀend of the arm, elbow), ankulos (c̄rooked, curved), ankula (ānchor). See אוּנְקָל. Derivative: עגן [II].

מָשִׁיחַ – Mashiach

מׁשׁח [I] to smear, anoint.
— **Qal** – מָשַׁח he smeared, anointed.
— **Niph.** – 1 נִמְשַׁח was anointed; MH 2 was smeared. [BAram. and Aram.-Syr. מְשַׁח (ħe smeared, anointed), Aram. מִשְׁחָא, Syr. מֶשְׁחָא (ōil), Ugar. mshḥ (to smash, shatter), Akka. mashā'u (to spread oil over), Arab. masaḥa (ħe stroked or wiped with the hand, anointed), Ethiop. masaḥ (ħe anointed, feasted, dined). cp. מָשְׁעִי.] Derivatives: מָשׁוּחַ, מִשְׁחָה, מָשְׁחָה, מָשִׁיחַ, מְשִׁיחָה הַמָּשְׁחוּת, מִמְשָׁח, תַּמְשִׁיחַ [I].

מָשִׁיחַ m.n. 1 the anointed (king or high priest). 2 'Messiah'. [From מׁשׁח [I] (= to anoint). cp. מְשִׁיחָא. cp. also 'Messiah' and 'Messias' in my CEDEL.] Derivatives: מְשִׁיחִי, שִׁיחוּת.

---
[6]Definitions from: Ernest Klein, 'A Comprehensive Etymological Dictionary of the Hebrew Language for Readers of English', Sefaria, accessed 9 May 2021, https://www.sefaria.org/Klein_Dictionary
Formatting changed to conform to book format: Ezra SIL SR for Hebrew, Helvetica for English.

נָגִיד – **Nagid**

נֶגֶד prep. & adv. in front of, before; opposite, against, contrary to; in the presence of. [Orig. a noun lit. meaning 'that which is high or conspicuous', from נגד (to be high, to be conspicuous).] Derivatives: נֶגְדִּי, נֶגְדָּה תִּנְגֹּבֶת.

נגד [I] to rise, be high, be conspicuous.
— **Qal** – נָגַד was against, opposed, contradicted.
— **Pi.** – נִגֵּד (of s.m.).
— **Pu.** – נֻגַּד (see מְנֻגָּד).
— **Hith.** – הִתְנַגֵּד was against, opposed, contradicted.
— **Hiph.** – הִגִּיד he made known, announced, declared, reported, told (orig. and properly, 'he placed a matter high or made it conspicuous before somebody').
— **Hoph.** – הֻגַּד was made known, was announced, was declared, was reported, was told. [Aram.-Syr. נְגַד (= he led, stretched, drew, dragged, attracted), נְגוֹדָא (leader, ruler), Arab. najd (= highland), najada (wās conspicuous; conquered), najuda, najida (wās courageous), najīd (nōble-minded). Denominated from נֶגֶד. cp. נגד [II].] Derivatives: מַגִּיד, הַנְגָּדָה, הַגָּדָה, הֶגֵּד, מִתְנַגֵּד, נָגִיד, נוֹגֵד, הִתְנַגְּדוּת, מְנֻגָּד.

נָגִיד m.n. 1 chief, leader, ruler. MH 2 noble, prince. NH 3 a wealthy man. [cp. Arab. najīd (nōble minded), and see נגד (= to rise, be high; to be conspicuous). For sense development cp. נָשִׂיא (prince, chief), lit.'one lifted up', from נשא (to lift). According to Barth the orig. meaning of נָגִיד is 'speaker', 'spokesman'. cp. נָשִׂיא (prince, chief), which may also have meant orig. 'speaker'.] Derivatives: נְגִידוּת, נְגִידִי.

Most people who hear or read the term עַד־מָשִׁיחַ נָגִיד – Ad Mashiach Nagid – **want to consider that it designates a person!** That is, in fact, how it is usually interpreted.

What if that interpretation is not the intended meaning – that it is misunderstood – simply because its words are typically interpreted as they are found in *other* textual contexts?

Is it at all possible that Gabriel's words were intended to be interpreted from the context in Daniel 9 only, rather than as other occurrences elsewhere?

Did the angel Gabriel know that his message to Daniel would be interpreted in many ways? Could that be one of the reasons he stressed that the vision was for a much later time?

If so, then did Gabriel foresee that his message would be construed so that it would even bring about Christianity?

Essentially, the words, Mashiach and Nagid, are most often understood to be an individual person.

To help look at these verses differently, I will try to give another sense, first by looking at Daniel 9:2, which is about Daniel's immediate concern regarding the fulfillment of the word of Yehovah to Jeremiah "that He would accomplish for the desolations of Yerushalam seventy years."

The following are the three verses in Jeremiah which speak about the seventy (70) years to which Daniel is concerned.

כה יא   וְהָיְתָה֩ כָּל־הָאָ֨רֶץ הַזֹּ֜את לְחָרְבָּ֗ה
לְשַׁמָּ֔ה וְעָבְד֞וּ הַגּוֹיִ֧ם הָאֵ֛לֶּה אֶת־מֶ֥לֶךְ בָּבֶ֖ל
שִׁבְעִ֥ים שָׁנָֽה׃

25 11   And this whole land shall be a desolation, and a waste; and these nations shall serve the king of Babylon seventy years.

יב   וְהָיָה כִמְלֹאות שִׁבְעִים שָׁנָה אֶפְקֹד
עַל־מֶלֶךְ־בָּבֶל וְעַל־הַגּוֹי הַהוּא נְאֻם־יְהוָה
אֶת־עֲוֺנָם וְעַל־אֶרֶץ כַּשְׂדִּים וְשַׂמְתִּי אֹתוֹ
לְשִׁמְמוֹת עוֹלָם:

12 And it shall come to pass, when seventy years are accomplished, that I will punish the king of Babylon, and that nation, saith Yehovah, for their iniquity, and the land of the Chaldeans; and I will make it perpetual desolations. [Jeremiah 25:11-12 The Pill Tanakh]

כט י   כִּי־כֹה אָמַר יְהוָה כִּי לְפִי מְלֹאת לְבָבֶל
שִׁבְעִים שָׁנָה אֶפְקֹד אֶתְכֶם וַהֲקִמֹתִי עֲלֵיכֶם
אֶת־דְּבָרִי הַטּוֹב לְהָשִׁיב אֶתְכֶם אֶל־הַמָּקוֹם
הַזֶּה:

29 10 For thus saith Yehovah: After seventy years are accomplished for Babylon, I will remember you, and perform My good word toward you, in causing you to return to this place. [Jeremiah 29:10 The Pill Tanakh]

The beginning of Daniel 9 appears to reference the passages in Jeremiah, as shown above.

ט א   בִּשְׁנַת אַחַת לְדָרְיָוֶשׁ בֶּן־אֲחַשְׁוֵרוֹשׁ מִזֶּרַע
מָדָי אֲשֶׁר הָמְלַךְ עַל מַלְכוּת כַּשְׂדִּים:

9 1 In the first year of Darius the son of Achashverosh, of the seed of the Medes, who was made king over the realm of the Chaldeans;

ב   בִּשְׁנַת אַחַת לְמָלְכוֹ אֲנִי דָּנִיֵּאל בִּינֹתִי בַּסְּפָרִים
מִסְפַּר הַשָּׁנִים אֲשֶׁר הָיָה דְבַר־יְהוָה אֶל־יִרְמְיָה
הַנָּבִיא לְמַלֹּאות לְחָרְבוֹת יְרוּשָׁלַ͏ִם שִׁבְעִים שָׁנָה:

2 in the first year of his reign I Daniel meditated in the books, over the number of the years, whereof the word of Yehovah came to Jeremiah the prophet, that He would accomplish for the desolations of Yerushalam seventy years. [Daniel 9:1-2 The Pill Tanakh]

I find it compelling that in the beginning of Daniel 9, Daniel is concerned about the time when the seventy (70) years of Jeremiah's prophecy would be complete.   However, when answering Daniel, **Gabriel uses the number seventy (70) in a different way as a means to express a greater event!**

Rather than responding to Daniel's specific meditation of when Jeremiah's prophecy would be fulfilled,   the angel Gabriel speaks about a general restoration to Yerushalam that would bring in "everlasting righteousness."

Gabriel Appears To Address <u>A</u> <u>Question</u> <u>Not</u> <u>Asked</u>!

In response to Daniel's meditation, the angel Gabriel doesn't directly provide an answer regarding his question about Jeremiah!

כד שָׁבֻעִים שִׁבְעִים נֶחְתַּךְ עַל־עַמְּךָ ׀ וְעַל־עִיר ט
קָדְשֶׁךָ לְכַלֵּא הַפֶּשַׁע וּלְהָתֵם חַטָּאת וּלְכַפֵּר עָוֹן
וּלְהָבִיא צֶדֶק עֹלָמִים וְלַחְתֹּם חָזוֹן וְנָבִיא וְלִמְשֹׁחַ
קֹדֶשׁ קָדָשִׁים:

9 24 Seventy weeks are decreed upon thy people and upon thy holy city, to finish the transgression, and to make an end of sin, and to forgive iniquity, and to bring in everlasting righteousness, and to seal vision and prophet, and to anoint the most holy place. [Daniel 9:24 The Pill Tanakh]

Where the verse begins שָׁבְעִים שִׁבְעִים, it is literally translated "Seventy Sevens," although it is often translated as "Seventy weeks," as shown in the text above. The common interpretation is seventy times seven years (70 x 7 = 490).

וְעַל־עִיר קָדְשֶׁךָ "and upon thy holy city" is no doubt referring to Yerusalam and the end of verse 24 ends with a reference to וְלִמְשֹׁחַ קֹדֶשׁ קָדָשִׁים: "and to anoint the most holy place," also known as the Holy of Holies!

קֹדֶשׁ — Kodesh [7]

קָדַשׁ to be holy, be sacred.
— **Qal** – 1 קָדַשׁ was set apart, was consecrated. **2** was forbidden.
— **Niph.** – 1 נִקְדַּשׁ was hallowed, was sanctified, **2** was consecrated, was dedicated.
— **Pi.** – 1 קִדֵּשׁ he hallowed, sanctified; **2** he dedicated; consecrated; **3** he declared holy; **4** he cleansed, purified; **5** he devoted, assigned; PBH **6** he sanctified the Sabbath or the festivals; PBH **7** he pronounced the benediction of Kiddush; PBH **8** he made something prohibited; PBH **9** he betrothed, wedded.
— **Pu.** – 1 קֻדַּשׁ was hallowed, was sanctified; **2** was dedicated was consecrated; PBH **3** was betrothed, was wedded.
— **Hith.** – 1 הִתְקַדֵּשׁ he kept himself separated, purified himself; **2** he became sanctified; **3** he prepared himself; PBH **4** it was forbidden (as food).
— **Hiph.** – 1 הִקְדִּישׁ he set apart as holy, devoted as holy; **2** he regarded as holy; **3** he designated, appointed; NH **4** he dedicated.
— **Hoph.** – 1 הֻקְדַּשׁ was set apart as holy, was devoted as holy; MH **2** was regarded as holy; NH **3** was designated, was appointed; NH **4** was dedicated. [Related to Ugar. qdsh (= sanctuary), Phoen. קדש (= holy), מקדש (= sanctuary, holy place), Aram.-Syr. קַדֵּשׁ (= he hallowed, sanctified, consecrated), Palm. קדש (= to sanctify, consecrate), Arab. qadusa (= was holy, was

---

[7] ibid

pure), quaddasa (= he hallowed, sanctified, consecrated; he went to Jerusalem), quds (= purity, holiness), al-quds (= Jerusalem; lit.: 'the holy place'), Akka. quddushu (= to cleanse, to hallow, sanctify,), Aram.–Syr. קְדְשָׁא (= ear or nose ring; orig. 'holy thing'). The orig. meaning of this base prob. was 'to separate'.] Derivatives: מִקְדָּשׁ, מְקֻדָּשׁ, קֹדֶשׁ, קֶדֶשׁ, קְדֵשָׁה, קְדֵשָׁה, קַדְשָׁא, קָדוֹשׁ, קָדוֹשׁ, קַדִּישׁ, הֶקְדֵּשׁ, הַקְדָּשָׁה, אַקְדָּשָׁה, הִתְקַדְּשׁוּת. cp. the second element in קַדְשְׁנוּן.

קֹדֶשׁ m.n. **1** holiness, sanctity. **2** a holy object. **3** a holy place. **4** the Holy Temple. [From קדשׁ cp. Aram. קוּדְשָׁא (= holiness), Syr. קוּדְשָׁא (= dedication, consecration), Ugar. qdsh (= holy place, sanctuary), qdsh (= a goddess), qdsht (name of a goddess).]

Interestingly, קֹדֶשׁ 'Kodesh' and its variations are typically translated as **"Holy."** In Daniel 9:24, the first instance in the phrase וְעַל־עִיר קָדְשֶׁךָ appears under the translation of **"and upon thy holy city,"** and the second instance appears at the end of the verse as :וְלִמְשֹׁחַ קֹדֶשׁ קָדָשִׁים, translated as **"and to anoint the most holy place."**

I believe that these two occurrences representing **"Holy"** are referring to **anointing Yerushalam, the <u>Holy</u> city, and anointing the <u>Holy</u> sanctuary** :וְלִמְשֹׁחַ קֹדֶשׁ קָדָשִׁים! In that sense, both Yerushalam and the Sanctuary are paired together in one place.

Where the end of the verse reads :וְלִמְשֹׁחַ קֹדֶשׁ קָדָשִׁים the word for **"anoint"** appears. **"Mashiach,"** in its simple rendering means "to anoint, anointed" but *in the next verse* it appears as עַד־מָשִׁיחַ נָגִיד **"unto Mashiach Nagid"** (Daniel 9:25).

I have mentioned, above, that I believe וְעַל־עִיר קָדְשֶׁךָ **the holy city of Yerushalam** is understood in the last phrase of verse 25: :וְלִמְשֹׁחַ קֹדֶשׁ קָדָשִׁים *(and to anoint the most holy place).*

I now consider the possibility that מָשִׁיחַ **Mashiach**, in Daniel 9, <u>IS NOT REFERRING TO A PERSON, BUT RATHER TO A PLACE:</u>

וְעַל־עִיר קָדְשֶׁ֫ךָ **THE HOLY CITY OF YERUSHALAM** and

וְלִמְשֹׁחַ קֹדֶשׁ קָדָשִׁים: **THE ANOINTED HOLY OF HOLIES!**

I believe that is because the וְעַל־עִיר קָדְשֶׁ֫ךָ the holy City of **Yerushalam is the subject of Daniel 9:24, which sets it up to be the intended subject of the subsequent verses!**

Look at Daniel 9:24–27 and consider וְעַל־עִיר קָדְשֶׁ֫ךָ
Yerushalam as the Holy City וְלִמְשֹׁחַ קֹדֶשׁ קָדָשִׁים: *and the*
Anointed Most Holy Place:

ט כד שָׁבֻעִים שִׁבְעִים נֶחְתַּ֣ךְ עַל־עַמְּךָ ו וְעַל־עִיר
קָדְשֶׁ֫ךָ לְכַלֵּ֣א הַפֶּ֫שַׁע וּלְהָתֵ֣ם חַטָּאות וּלְכַפֵּ֣ר עָוֹן
וּלְהָבִ֣יא צֶ֣דֶק עֹֽלָמִ֑ים וְלַחְתֹּם֙ חָז֣וֹן וְנָבִ֔יא וְלִמְשֹׁ֖חַ
קֹ֥דֶשׁ קָֽדָשִֽׁים׃

9 24 Seventy weeks are decreed upon thy people and upon thy holy city, to finish the transgression, and to make an end of sin, and to forgive iniquity, and to bring in everlasting righteousness, and to seal vision and prophet, and to anoint the most holy place.

כה וְתֵדַ֣ע וְתַשְׂכֵּ֗ל מִן־מֹצָ֣א דָבָ֔ר לְהָשִׁיב֙ וְלִבְנ֣וֹת
יְרֽוּשָׁלִַ֗ם עַד־מָשִׁ֣יחַ נָגִ֔יד שָׁבֻעִ֖ים שִׁבְעָ֑ה וְשָׁבֻעִ֞ים
שִׁשִּׁ֣ים וּשְׁנַ֗יִם תָּשׁוּב֙ וְנִבְנְתָה֙ רְח֣וֹב וְחָר֔וּץ וּבְצ֖וֹק
הָעִתִּֽים׃

25 Know therefore and discern, that from the going forth of the word to restore and to build Yerushalam unto Mashiach nagid shall be seven weeks; and for sixty-two weeks, it shall be built again, with broad place and moat, but in troublous times.

כו וְאַחֲרֵי הַשָּׁבֻעִים שִׁשִּׁים וּשְׁנַיִם יִכָּרֵת מָשִׁיחַ
וְאֵין לוֹ וְהָעִיר וְהַקֹּדֶשׁ יַשְׁחִית עַם נָגִיד הַבָּא וְקִצּוֹ
בַשֶּׁטֶף וְעַד קֵץ מִלְחָמָה נֶחֱרֶצֶת שֹׁמֵמוֹת:

26   And after the sixty-two weeks shall Mashiach be cut off, and be no more; and the people of the ruler that shall come shall destroy the city and the sanctuary; but his end shall be with a flood; and unto the end of the war desolations are determined.

כז וְהִגְבִּיר בְּרִית לָרַבִּים שָׁבוּעַ אֶחָד וַחֲצִי
הַשָּׁבוּעַ יַשְׁבִּית זֶבַח וּמִנְחָה וְעַל כְּנַף שִׁקּוּצִים
מְשֹׁמֵם וְעַד־כָּלָה וְנֶחֱרָצָה תִּתַּךְ עַל־שֹׁמֵם:

27   And he shall make a firm covenant with many for one week; and for half of the week he shall cause the sacrifice and the offering to cease; and upon the wing of detestable things shall be that which causeth appalment; and that until the extermination wholly determined be poured out upon that which causeth appalment.'

If you read those verses, my hope is that you gave consideration that קֹדֶשׁ 'Kodesh – Holy' *and* מָשִׁיחַ — 'Mashiach – anointed' can, indeed, actually both be about וְעַל־עִיר קָדְשֶׁךָ Yerushalam as the Holy City and וְלִמְשֹׁחַ קֹדֶשׁ קָדָשִׁים: the Anointed Most Holy Place within the city of Yerushalam!

Revisiting Daniel's '62 Weeks'

During the Roman conquest, Pompey entered (63 BCE) the Holy of Holies but left the Temple intact. In 54 BCE, however, Crassus plundered the Temple treasury. Of major importance was the rebuilding of the Second Temple begun by Herod the Great, king (37 BCE–4 CE) of Judaea.

Construction began in 20 BCE and lasted for 46 years. The area of the Temple Mount was doubled and surrounded by a retaining wall with gates. The Temple was raised, enlarged, and faced with white stone. The new Temple square served as a gathering place, and its porticoes sheltered merchants and money changers. A stone fence (*soreg*) and a rampart (*hel*) surrounded the consecrated area forbidden to Gentiles. The Temple proper began, on the east, with the Court of Women, each side of which had a gate and each corner of which had a chamber. This court was named for a surrounding balcony on which women observed the annual celebration of Sukkoth. The western gate of the court, approached by a semicircular staircase, led to the Court of the Israelites, that portion of the Court of Priests open to all male Jews. Surrounding the inner sanctuary, the Court of Priests contained the sacrificial altar and a copper laver for priestly ablutions. This court was itself surrounded by a wall broken with gates and chambers. The Temple sanctuary building was wider in front than in the rear; its eastern facade had two pillars on either side of the gate to the entrance hall. Within the hall, a great gate led to the sanctuary, at the western end of which was the Holy of Holies.

The Herodian Temple was again the centre of Israelite life. It was not only the focus of religious ritual but also the repository of the Holy Scriptures and other national literature and the meeting place of the Sanhedrin, the highest court of Jewish law during the Roman period. The rebellion against Rome that began in 66 CE soon focused on the Temple and effectively ended with the Temple's destruction on the 9th/10th of Av, 70 CE.[8]

כו וְאַחֲרֵי הַשָּׁבֻעִים֙ שִׁשִּׁים֙ וּשְׁנַ֔יִם יִכָּרֵ֥ת מָשִׁ֖יחַ וְאֵ֣ין ל֑וֹ וְהָעִ֣יר וְהַקֹּ֗דֶשׁ יַ֠שְׁחִית עַ֣ם נָגִ֤יד הַבָּא֙ וְקִצּ֣וֹ בַשֶּׁ֔טֶף וְעַד֙ קֵ֣ץ מִלְחָמָ֔ה נֶחֱרֶ֖צֶת שֹׁמֵמֽוֹת׃

9 <u>26</u> And after the sixty-two weeks shall Mashiach be cut off, and be no more; and the people of the ruler that shall come shall destroy the city and the sanctuary; but his end shall be with a flood; and unto the end of the war desolations are determined.

[Daniel 9:26 The Pill Tanakh]

[8]The Editors of Encyclopaedia Britannica, 'Temple of Jerusalem,' Britannica, Last updated 18 Aug 2024, https://www.britannica.com/topic/Temple-of-Jerusalem.

In the first chapter of this book, I made the following statements:

> It is known from recorded history that the seven weeks (49 years) to the building of Yerushalam was fulfilled (Daniel 9:25). Cyrus is understood to have given the 'דבר ~ Devar (word)' to return to and build Yerushalam at around the year **538.**
>
> ...
>
> Nevertheless, by looking at the date of "the word" from Cyrus, *if* **it was around the 538 BCE,** then 49 years later (7 weeks / 7 sevens) would have brought us to around the date of **489 BCE** when returning to and building Yerushalam would have begun. **If we then subtract 434 years (62 x 7),** that would bring us to about the year **55 BCE.**

In the above quote from Encyclopaedia Britannica, they mentioned:

> During the Roman conquest, Pompey entered (63 BCE) the Holy of Holies but left the Temple intact. In 54 BCE, however, Crassus plundered the Temple treasury. Of major importance was the rebuilding of the Second Temple begun by Herod the Great, king (37 BCE–4 CE) of Judaea.
>
> **"... Pompey entered (63 BCE) the Holy of Holies but left the Temple intact. In 54 BCE, however, Crassus plundered the Temple treasury."**

You might note that, in my calculations, I came to '*about the year 55 BCE.* '55 BCE' is rather near, i.e. 'within striking distance,' to '54 BCE' as stated when Crassus plundered the treasury!

If עַד־מָשִׁיחַ נָגִיד **is** the *anointed* city of Yerushalam and is associatated as (מָשִׁיחַ **Mashiach,) the subject of Daniel 9:24-27,** and not *a person,* then those dates come quite close in marking the time of the end of the 62 weeks along with the chaos that came about at that time regarding *the city of Yerushalam.*

With all of these things under consideration, I am now of the opinion that, as directed by the angel Gabriel, Daniel's מָשִׁיחַ נָגִיד *Mashiach Nagid* **is the Holy city of Yerushalam!**

מָשִׁיחַ נָגִיד *Mashiach Nagid,* from the definitions, can be understood to be **'the conspicuous (nagid) – anointed one (Mashiach),'** rather than, 'for Mashiach to be a person!' As such, in verse 24, the two phrases וְעַל־עִיר קָדְשֶׁךָ **(upon thy holy city)** and וְלִמְשֹׁחַ קֹדֶשׁ קָדָשִׁים: **('and to anoint the most holy place.')** may also be considered to be not only the **intended subject** of Daniel 9:25, but the underlying theme of *Gabriel's* answer to Daniel's prayer — indeed, the entire prophetic discourse!

Returning to *the end* of Daniel's '62 Weeks'

The first part of the quote from Encyclopaedia Britannica, says:

> During the Roman conquest, Pompey entered (63 BCE) the Holy of Holies but left the Temple intact. In 54 BCE, however, Crassus plundered the Temple treasury. Of major importance was the rebuilding of the Second Temple begun by Herod the Great, king (37 BCE–4 CE) of Judaea.
> Construction began in 20 BCE and lasted for 46 years. The area of the Temple Mount was doubled and surrounded by a retaining wall with gates. The Temple was raised, enlarged, and faced with white stone.   The new Temple square served as a gathering place, and its porticoes sheltered merchants and money changers. ...

In human terms,

'Herod's Temple' was a magnificent structure.

However, I believe that **'Herod's Temple'** *was an abomination!*

The **sin of idolatry** is well expressed as the second commandment among *The Ten Commandments!*

לֹא
יִהְיֶה לְךָ אֱלֹהִים אֲחֵרִים עַל־
פָּנַי לֹא תַעֲשֶׂה לְךָ פֶסֶל וְכֹל
תְּמוּנָה אֲשֶׁר בַּשָּׁמַיִם מִמַּעַל
וַאֲשֶׁר בָּאָרֶץ מִתַּחַת וַאֲשֶׁר
בַּמַּיִם מִתַּחַת לָאָרֶץ לֹא
תִשְׁתַּחֲוֶה לָהֶם וְלֹא תָעַבְדֵם
כִּי אָנֹכִי יְהוָה אֱלֹהֶיךָ אֵל
קַנָּא פֹּקֵד עֲוֹן אָבֹת עַל־
בָּנִים עַל־שִׁלֵּשִׁים וְעַל־
רִבֵּעִים לְשֹׂנְאָי׃

ב ג לֹא יִהְיֶה־לְךָ אֱלֹהִים אֲחֵרִים עַל־פָּנָי לֹא
תַעֲשֶׂה־לְךָ פֶסֶל ׀ וְכָל־תְּמוּנָה אֲשֶׁר בַּשָּׁמַיִם ׀
מִמַּעַל וַאֲשֶׁר בָּאָרֶץ מִתַּחַת וַאֲשֶׁר בַּמַּיִם ׀
מִתַּחַת לָאָרֶץ לֹא־תִשְׁתַּחֲוֶה לָהֶם וְלֹא תָעָבְדֵם
כִּי אָנֹכִי יְהוָה אֱלֹהֶיךָ אֵל קַנָּא פֹּקֵד עֲוֹן אָבֹת
עַל־בָּנִים עַל־שִׁלֵּשִׁים וְעַל־רִבֵּעִים לְשֹׂנְאָי׃

20 3 Thou shalt have no other gods before
Me. Thou shalt not make unto thee a graven
image, nor any manner of likeness, of any
thing that is in heaven above, or that is in the
earth beneath, or that is in the water under
the earth; thou shalt not bow down unto
them, nor serve them; for I Yehovah thy God
am a jealous God, visiting the iniquity of the
fathers upon the children unto the third and

fourth generation of them that hate Me;

[Exodus 20:3 The Pill Tanakh]

In the same chapter containing **The Ten Commandments** there are two verses (Exodus 20:19-20) which appear before the last verse (v21). I believe, those verses are indicative of how Yehovah intends to help keep **His people** from worshipping the Creation, rather than the Creator! In a nutshell, it is an expression of keeping away from the sin of idolatry, as shown in Exodus 20:3 at the beginning of the chapter.

כ יט מִזְבַּח אֲדָמָה תַּעֲשֶׂה־לִּי וְזָבַחְתָּ עָלָיו
אֶת־עֹלֹתֶיךָ וְאֶת־שְׁלָמֶיךָ אֶת־צֹאנְךָ וְאֶת־בְּקָרֶךָ
בְּכָל־הַמָּקוֹם אֲשֶׁר אַזְכִּיר אֶת־שְׁמִי אָבוֹא אֵלֶיךָ
וּבֵרַכְתִּיךָ:

20 19 An altar of earth thou shalt make unto Me, and shalt sacrifice thereon thy burnt-offerings, and thy peace-offerings, thy sheep, and thine oxen; in every place where I cause My name to be mentioned I will come unto thee and bless thee.

כ וְאִם־מִזְבַּח אֲבָנִים תַּעֲשֶׂה־לִּי לֹא־תִבְנֶה אֶתְהֶן
גָּזִית כִּי חַרְבְּךָ הֵנַפְתָּ עָלֶיהָ וַתְּחַלְלֶהָ:

20 And if thou make Me an altar of stone, thou shalt not build it of hewn stones; for if thou lift up thy tool upon it, thou hast profaned it. [Exodus 20:19-20 The Pill Tanakh]

Again, in my opinion, although in human terms Herod's Temple was magnificent, I believe it was actually an abomination! Not only was it beautiful, it was also larger than Solomon's Temple and the Temple of Ezra and Nehemia. However, that "beautification" far exceeded the simpler, though elegant, structure Yehovah had tasked Solomon with building. I think that it follows the sentiment described in Exodus 20:20, **And if you make Me an altar of** *stone, thou shalt not build it of hewn stones; for if thou lift up thy tool upon it, thou has profaned it.*

Can the unusual wording in the last verse of Daniel 9 be talking about the time of the Romans entering the Temple prior to the building of Herod's 'Magnificent Temple,' **which I believe was an abomination?**

כז וְהִגְבִּיר בְּרִית לָרַבִּים שָׁבוּעַ אֶחָד וַחֲצִי שׁ
הַשָּׁבוּעַ יַשְׁבִּית | זֶבַח וּמִנְחָה וְעַל כְּנַף שִׁקּוּצִים
מְשֹׁמֵם וְעַד־כָּלָה וְנֶחֱרָצָה תִּתַּךְ עַל־שֹׁמֵם:

9 _27_ And he shall make a firm covenant with many for one week; and for half of the week he shall cause the sacrifice and the offering to cease; and upon the wing of detestable things shall be that which causeth appalment; and that until the extermination wholly determined be poured out upon that which causeth appalment.'

[Daniel 9:27 The Pill Tanakh]

Summary

In this chapter, I gave definitions of לְהָשִׁיב 'L'hashiv,' (to return to) and עַד־מָשִׁיחַ נָגִיד 'Ad Mashiach Nagid,' (unto Mashiach nagid) and קֹדֶשׁ 'Kodesh' (holy), which should help in the understanding of this critical text of Daniel 9:25.

Further, I showed how that there is a possibility that the Holy city of Yerusahalam may be considered *"the conspicuous anointed"* (**The Mashiach nagid**).

I finished with "The 62 Weeks," showing in the **55–54 BCE** timeline that the Temple was certainly desecrated by the Romans

(Pompey and Crassus) in not only entering the Holy of Holies but also plundering the treasury.

Further, I associated Herod's attempt to rebuild the Temple into a beautiful edifice **could have actually been seen as** *an abomination* **in the eyes of the Almighty God (Yehovah)!**

גַּבְרִיאֵל יָדַע

Gabriel Knew!

Did the angel Gabriel know that his message to Daniel would be interpreted, <u>and</u> <u>even</u> <u>misinterpreted</u>, in many ways?

Could that be one of the reasons he stressed that the vision was to be sealed for a much later time?

If so, then could he have already foreseen that his message would be construed that it would even bring about Christianity?

In previous chapters, I brought about the idea that words and phrases, such as עַד־מָשִׁיחַ נָגִיד 'Ad Mashiach Nagid' have been understood, from other Biblical contexts, to be about **'a person.'**

However, within the context of Daniel 9:24-25, I posited the idea that Gabriel's discourse was actually about **the Holy City of Yerushalam and the Most Holy, Anointed, Place!**

I showed that within the Hebrew grammar of Daniel 9:25, there is absolutely no doubt that עַד־מָשִׁיחַ נָגִיד 'Ad Mashiach Nagid' can only be associated with the forty–nine (49) years from the word 'to return to and build Yerushalam,' <u>and</u> <u>NOT</u> <u>with</u> <u>the</u> <u>end</u> <u>of</u> <u>the</u> <u>sixty–two</u> <u>(62)</u> <u>weeks</u> <u>of</u> <u>years</u> <u>(483)</u>, <u>as</u> <u>found</u> <u>in</u> <u>the</u> <u>second</u> <u>part</u> <u>of</u> <u>the</u> <u>verse</u>.

Thus, based upon a clear understanding of the Hebrew of the Masoretic text, within the prophetic timeline it is absolutely **impossible** for **Jesus (as the Messiah)** to have come at the end of the 62 weeks (Daniel 9:25b). By interpreting the verse correctly, "whoever עַד־מָשִׁיחַ נָגִיד 'Ad Mashiach Nagid'" would turn out to be, would have to have come at the time of returning to and building Yerushalam — at the end of the forty–nine (49) years!

Yet, despite misconstruing the discourse of the angel Gabriel and the natural grammar of the Hebrew text, Christianity was still established and became a major world religion, <u>helping</u> <u>to</u> <u>bring</u> <u>about</u> <u>the</u> <u>universal</u> <u>knowledge</u> <u>of</u> <u>The</u> <u>One</u> <u>God</u>!

Subsequently, even in our day and age many Christians believe **that since 'they are seeds of Abraham by faith'** [1]   that

---

[1] In Romans 11:11–24 Paul compares Israel to the natural branches of a cultivated olive tree and the Gentile believers to the branches of a wild olive tree. Some of the natural branches (Israel) were broken off, and the wild branches (Gentiles) were grafted in (verse 17). The Gentiles, then, have been made partakers of the promises and inherit the blessings of God's salvation.

It is important to understand how God called Israel to be His people and how they failed to fulfill that calling. As the seed of Abraham, the children of Israel were chosen by God to be a separate people, holy to the Lord. God's design was for them to be a light to the Gentiles so that they, too, might know God (Genesis 18:17–19; Isaiah 42, 49). Instead, the Israelites chased foreign gods and betrayed their calling (Ezekiel 23; Hosea 11). But God, who knew they would do this, had already promised to restore His kingdom to Israel after they rebelled and then eventually repented (Deuteronomy 30:1–10). So God sent His Son, preceded by a forerunner, to invite Israel to "repent, for the Kingdom of heaven is at hand" (Matthew 3:2; 4:17).

However, when Jesus revealed Himself as the promised Davidic King who would restore Israel (Matthew 11−12; Acts 3:19−22), He was rejected by the Jews, exactly as Isaiah had prophesied (Isaiah 52−53). Jesus therefore called His disciples to fulfill Abraham's commission to bless the nations (Genesis 12:2–3) by preaching the gospel of the Kingdom to all nations until the end of this age (Matthew 28:18–20). Paul thus preached the gospel of the Kingdom to the Jews and was repeatedly rejected (Acts 13−28); in consequence, Paul brought the good news to the Gentiles, who in turn became Abraham's spiritual seed by faith and heirs of the promises to Abraham and his seed (Galatians 3−4). This is what Paul meant in Romans 11 by the Gentiles being "grafted" into the "olive tree" and nourished by the "root" (the promises to Abraham). The tree thus signifies the collective people of God; the "wild branches" grafted in are Gentile believers; the "natural branches" that are cut off are the Jews in unbelief. Jewish believers remain in the tree but are joined with Gentiles and "made" into a "new body," the Church (Ephesians 2:11–22).

Paul anticipated a question that would surely arise among his Gentile readers: "I say then, have they stumbled that they should fall?" (Romans 11:11)—Gentile believers would be tempted to dismiss Israel because it appeared they would never recover. Even today, there are those who advocate supersessionism or replacement theology, which holds that the Church has completely replaced Israel and will inherit the promises to be fulfilled only in a spiritual sense. In other words, according to this view, ethnic Israel is forever excluded from the promises—the Jews will not literally inherit the Promised Land. What then would happen to Israel? What about the Old Testament prophecies that Israel as a nation would repent and be re–gathered to the land in the last days as a permanent possession (Deuteronomy 30:1–10)?

...

Got Questions, "Has the church been grafted in Israel's place?", accessed 21 Nov 2024, https://www.gotquestions.org/grafted-Israel.html.

self–entitles them to consider that *__somehow__* *__they__* *__now__* *__have__* *__become__* *__the__* *__new__* *__Jewish__* *__people__* — that they have **supplanted, i.e. replaced, ethnic Israel!**

Where did that ***arrogance*** originate? I believe it is from none other than the self–proclaimed apostle Paul !

Know ye therefore that they which are of faith, the same are the children of Abraham. [Galatians 3:7 KJV]

Ironically, that faith of Abraham began with the **original covenant of circumcision** that אֱלֹהִים Elohim (God) made with Abraham!

יז ט   וַיֹּאמֶר אֱלֹהִים אֶל־אַבְרָהָם וְאַתָּה
אֶת־בְּרִיתִי תִשְׁמֹר אַתָּה וְזַרְעֲךָ אַחֲרֶיךָ לְדֹרֹתָם:

17 9 And God said unto Abraham: 'And as for thee, thou shalt keep My covenant, thou, and thy seed after thee throughout their generations.

י   זֹאת בְּרִיתִי אֲשֶׁר תִּשְׁמְרוּ בֵּינִי וּבֵינֵיכֶם וּבֵין
זַרְעֲךָ אַחֲרֶיךָ הִמּוֹל לָכֶם כָּל־זָכָר:

10 This is My covenant, which ye shall keep, between Me and you and thy seed after thee: every male among you shall be circumcised.
...

יד   וְעָרֵל ׀ זָכָר אֲשֶׁר לֹא־יִמּוֹל אֶת־בְּשַׂר עָרְלָתוֹ
וְנִכְרְתָה הַנֶּפֶשׁ הַהִוא מֵעַמֶּיהָ אֶת־בְּרִיתִי הֵפַר:

14 And the uncircumcised male who is not circumcised in the flesh of his foreskin, that soul shall be cut off from his people; he hath broken My covenant.'
[Genesis 17:9-10,14 The Pill Tanakh]

No doubt but the covenant of circumcision is binding upon the seed of Abraham, along with other commandments that many of those who consider that they are children of Abraham by faith (Christians) conveniently ignore!

Unfortunately, so many of those people consider that they are the inheritors of all of the positive promises that Yehovah gave to the ethnic Israelite people (actual Jews), but they sincerely believe that they can disregard obeying all the laws, statutes and commandments required to receive those promises! [2]

In one of my books[3] I talked about Talmudism, the Jewish religion based upon rabbinic writings, which **euphemistically** refers to themselves as **Torah Observant.** When they say 'Torah Observant,' they are not talking about the written Torah of Moses, but rather their own writings (i.e. the Talmud, the Oral Torah)!

In a similar way, when Christians speak of Jesus, **many of them consider that he is actually Elohim—God.** When they see 'God' or even an 'angel' mentioned in the Jewish Scriptures (they call it 'The Old Testament'), **they automatically mentally insert 'Jesus' into the text!**

As an example, many of them actually believe that the fourth person in the midst of the fiery furnace of Nebuchadnezzar is absolutely Jesus![4]

Ironically, Daniel 3 does not give any indication of who the fourth person in the midst of the fiery furnace is! Those who interpret the text in that way base much of their belief system upon these kinds of cavalier assumptions without having interpretive integrity and a

---

[2]Here are just a few of the verses in the Jewish Scriptures which speak about keeping the commandments and the accompanying results from doing so: Exodus 31:12-17, Leviticus 18:4-5, Deuteronomy 5:24-31, 6:1-25, 8:1-2, 10:12-13, 11:26-28, 12:23-28, 30:10-20.

[3]Robert M. Pill, ''Jesus Cannot Be The Jewish Messiah*,'' (Robert M. Pill, Kerrville, TX), pp 83-98.

[4]See Daniel 3 in the Jewish Scriptures. If you search on the internet with the words **"Jesus in the fiery furnace"** you will find a plethora of sites affirming that Jesus (pre-incarnate or otherwise) is, indeed, the fourth person in the midst of the fiery furnace, along with Shadrach, Meshach and Abednego!

genuine Scriptural authority of to do so.

However, if Christianity had never come about, I am not quite sure that the knowledge of the אֱלֹהִים Elohim (God) of אַבְרָהָם Abraham, יִצְחָק Isaac and יַעֲקֹב Jacob would have been universally known as it is now!

In spite of its many flaws from a Scriptural point of view (measured against the Hebrew–language based Jewish Scriptures), the idea of **One God,** historically speaking, was mostly promulgated through the advent of the Christian religion.

Speaking in strictly human terms, I would be bold enough to say that the religion of Muhammad probably would not have come about without having been preceded by Christianity.

The Muslim religion (Islam) has also greatly contributed to **the knowledge of the Almighty God** among peoples who otherwise may not have been exposed to Him!

To reiterate, **I believe that the angel Gabriel absolutely knew that his words to Daniel would be** *misinterpreted* to help bring about 'the religion about Jesus' and subsequently to 'the religion of Muhammad.' Christianity and Islam brought about the knowledge of the One God to the world at large.

Culturally speaking, both Christian and Islamic religions have greatly contributed to the Renaissance of universal knowledge, especially in the arts and sciences. No doubt but the world has greatly benefitted from them!

Of course, that does not excuse those religious institutions and their adherents from persecuting the Israelite, Jewish people throughout the ages. Neither does it give them a license to proclaim that they have supplanted the Israelite, Jewish people as the people of Yehovah.

It is my belief that the words of the angel Gabriel, particularly as recorded in Daniel 9:25, have previously been interpreted as they appear in other Scriptural contexts. I have come to believe that those words were specifically given by Gabriel in response to Daniel's prayer of meditation earlier in that chapter, and should be interpreted independently of other contexts.

I consider that Gabriel absolutely knew that his words would be misunderstood!

As a result, Gabriel's words to Daniel were used as a basis for the foundation of which later Christian expositors justified their belief that Gabriel was prophesying about the time frame for the coming of *The Jewish Messiah!* Thus, *their misconstruction of the Jewish text* conveniently coincided with the advent of the life and times of Jesus of Nazareth!

Again, *I believe that Gabriel was well aware that his words were going to be misinterpreted.* He knew that interpreters would try to understand his words not just by understanding their definitions as presented in other contexts, which might identify Mashiach with a person rather than the Holy city of Yerushalam and the most Holy place, but also by misunderstanding the grammar of the Hebrew language to create a timeline for a person they considered to be The Messiah, which is absolutely inconsistent with the plain and simple meaning of the Hebrew text!

So, What Was The Result Of Those Misinterpretations?

No doubt, but much of the world has come to the knowledge of The One God with the advent of both the religions of Christianity and Islam!

I do not believe that Judaism, by itself, would have resulted in the universal belief in and knowledge of the One God!

The following are several prophetic passages, among many in the Jewish Scriptures, which speak about that transformation!

ב יד כִּי תִּמָּלֵא הָאָרֶץ לָדַעַת אֶת־כְּבוֹד
יְהֹוָה כַּמַּיִם יְכַסּוּ עַל־יָם:

2 14 For the earth shall be filled with the knowledge of the glory of Yehovah, as the waters cover the sea.

[Habakkuk 2:14 The Pill Tanakh]

ד א וְהָיָה ׀ בְּאַחֲרִית הַיָּמִים יִהְיֶה הַר
בֵּית־יְהֹוָה נָכוֹן בְּרֹאשׁ הֶהָרִים וְנִשָּׂא הוּא
מִגְּבָעוֹת וְנָהֲרוּ עָלָיו עַמִּים:

4 1 But in the end of days it shall come to pass, that the mountain of Yehovah's house shall be established as the top of the mountains, and it shall be exalted above the hills; and peoples shall flow unto it.

ב וְהָלְכוּ גּוֹיִם רַבִּים וְאָמְרוּ לְכוּ ׀ וְנַעֲלֶה
אֶל־הַר־יְהֹוָה וְאֶל־בֵּית אֱלֹהֵי יַעֲקֹב וְיוֹרֵנוּ
מִדְּרָכָיו וְנֵלְכָה בְּאֹרְחֹתָיו כִּי מִצִּיּוֹן תֵּצֵא
תוֹרָה וּדְבַר־יְהֹוָה מִירוּשָׁלָ͏ִם:

2 And many nations shall go and say: 'Come ye, and let us go up to the mountain of Yehovah, and to the house of the God of Jacob; and He will teach us of His ways, and we will walk in His paths'; for out of Zion shall go forth the Torah, and the word of Yehovah from Yerushalam.

ג וְשָׁפַט בֵּין עַמִּים רַבִּים וְהוֹכִיחַ לְגוֹיִם

עֲצֻמִים עַד־רָחֹוק וְכִתְּתוּ חַרְבֹתֵיהֶם
לְאִתִּים וַחֲנִיתֹתֵיהֶם לְמַזְמֵרֹות לֹא־יִשְׂאוּ
גֹוי אֶל־גֹּוי חֶרֶב וְלֹא־יִלְמְדוּן עֹוד
מִלְחָמָה׃

3 And He shall judge between many peoples, and shall decide concerning mighty nations afar off; and they shall beat their swords into plowshares, and their spears into pruninghooks; nation shall not lift up sword against nation, neither shall they learn war any more.
[Micah 4:1-3 The Pill Tanakh]

Gabriel Knew!

Had Christianity never come about, I do not believe that the universal knowledge of the אֱלֹהִים Elohim (God) of אַבְרָהָם Abraham, יִצְחָק Isaac and יַעֲקֹב Jacob would have been universally known as it is now!

2 14 For the earth shall be filled with the knowledge of the glory of Yehovah, as the waters cover the sea. [Habakkuk 2:14 The Pill Tanakh]

Biblical Judaism

Biblical? Judaism?
Are These Terms Mutually Exclusive?

Obviously, **'Biblical'** relates to **'the Bible,'** a more generic, universal term for what is typically understood as the **Judeo–Christian Scriptures.** Both Jewish and Christian groups often refer to the Scriptures as **'The Bible.'**

However, I take umbrage with that definition because I consider the Jewish Scriptures and the Christian Scriptures as distinct. Christians often refer to the Jewish Scriptures as 'The Old Testament.' When I talk about the Jewish Scriptures, I am referring to the Hebrew–language based Jewish Scriptures, the source of which is The Leningrad Codex, aka The Masoretic Text.

What Is Judaism?

Judaism (the Jewish Religion) is defined as the totality of beliefs and practices of the Jewish people, as given by **G-d** and recorded in the **Torah** (Hebrew Bible) and subsequent sacred writings of Judaism (Talmud and Kabbalah).

Judaism mandates that Jewish people follow the *mitzvot,* Divine commandments. Major mitzvot include resting and celebrating on Shabbat and Jewish holidays, eating kosher foods, studying Torah, and living in accordance with its teachings.

Judaism is based on the G-d's covenant with the forefathers and the revelation at Sinai, when He chose the Jewish people as His own and they committed to follow the Torah.[1]

---

[1] Menachem Posner, 'What Is Judaism?,' Chabad.org, accessed 12 Dec 2024, https://www.chabad.org/library/article_cdo/aid/3710122/jewish/What-Is-Judaism.htm.

In my opinion, when most people think about Judaism, the above description seems to represent their general understanding.

I once had a colleague that although he thought that the Jewish religion was based upon the Torah, **he believed that the Torah and the Talmud were the same thing!** That general ignorance is probably indicative of how many folks have been lead to believe that Talmudic Judaism is often thought to be *the true Judaism!*

Then What Is *True* Biblical Judaism?
Karaite Judaism!

Karaite Judaism or Karaism (also spelt Qaraite Judaism or Qaraism), is a Jewish religious movement characterized by the recognition of the Tanakh alone as its supreme authority in Halakha (Jewish religious law) and theology. It is distinct from mainstream Rabbinic Judaism, which considers the Oral Torah, as codified in the Talmud and subsequent works, to be authoritative interpretations of the Torah. Karaites maintain that all of the divine commandments handed down to Moses by God were recorded in the written Torah without additional Oral Law or explanation. As a result, Karaite Jews do not accept as binding the written collections of the oral tradition in the Midrash or Talmud.

During the 9th century C.E., a number of sects arose that denied the existence of oral Torah. These sects came to be known as Karaites (literally, People of the Scripture), and they were distinguished from the Rabbanites or Rabbinical Judaism.

The Karaites believed in strict interpretation of the literal text of the scripture, without rabbinical interpretation. They believed that rabbinical law was not part of an oral tradition that had been handed down from G-d, nor was it inspired by G-d, but was an original work of the sages. As such, rabbinical teachings are subject to the flaws of any document written by mere mortals.

The difference between Rabbanites and Karaites that is most commonly noted is in regard to the Sabbath: the Karaites noted that the Bible specifically prohibits lighting a flame on the Sabbath, so they kept their houses dark on the sabbath. The Rabbanites, on the other hand, relied upon rabbinical interpretation that allowed us to leave burning a flame that was ignited before the sabbath. Karaites also prohibited sexual intercourse on the sabbath, while Rabbanites considered the sabbath to be the best time for sexual intercourse. The Karaites also follow a slightly different calendar than the Rabbanites.

According to the Karaites, this movement at one time attracted as much as 40 percent of the Jewish people. Today, Karaites are a very small minority, and most Rabbinical Jews do not even know that they exist. A Karaite community existed in Egypt until the Six Day War A somewhat sizable community still lives in Los Angeles.[2]

I have mentioned elsewhere that I also consider myself to be a Karaite Jew! As spoken in the quote above, I recognize the Tanakh[3] (Jewish Scriptures based upon the ancient handwritten Leningrad Codex) alone as the supreme authority in Halakha and theology.

In my first book,[4] I focused on how that the Leningrad Codex, also known as The Masoretic Text, **is claimed to be the source for the ancient Jewish Scriptures of both Jewish and Christian**

---

[2]Jewish Virtual Library, 'Jewish Concepts: Karaites', accessed 13 Dec 2024, https://www.jewishvirtuallibrary.org/karaites.

[3]TaNaKh is an acronym which stands for Torah, Neviim (Prophets), and Ketuvim (Writings). Together, these three sections comprise the entire Jewish Scriptures, what Christians refer to as 'The Old Testament.'

[4]Robert M. Pill, 'The Real God Code: The Ten Commandments In The Leningrad Codex,' (Kerrville, TX, Robert M. Pill, 2021).

Bibles, *but* *absolutely* *none* *actually* *honor* *the* *integrity* *of* *the* *verse* *endings* *of* *the* *Ten* *Commandments* *of* *Exodus* *20!*

As an example, **the actual Leningrad Codex places the Ten Commandments of Exodus 20 in verses 1-12.** Other **Jewish Bibles use 14 verses,** breaking up the larger verses and combining the smaller ones. **Christian Bibles use 17 verses** to express the same section. **My question is, "Why do they claim The Masoretic Text as their source but they do not honor its clear verse separations for 'The Ten Commandments'?"**

To expand upon the title of this chapter, **Biblical Judaism,** I will provide a discussion related to the Ten Commandments and its universal importance!

The Ten Commandments
Two Perspectives

I am providing a couple of quotations about The Ten Commandments, first from a Jewish perspective, then a Christian (Roman Catholic). I chose these two sources because they seem to represent general views from each group.

As a disclaimer, I do not want to give the impression that these are my views. I want to emphasize that these are the views of the respective parties. I just want to present them to show common views on the subject.

A Jewish View

Aseret ha–Dibrot: עֲשֶׂרֶת הַדִּבְּרוֹת
The Ten Commandments

According to Jewish tradition, G-d gave the Jewish people 613 mitzvot (commandments). All 613 of those mitzvot are equally sacred, equally binding and equally the word of G-d. All of these mitzvot are treated as equally important, because human beings, with our limited understanding of the universe, have no way of knowing which mitzvot are more important in the eyes of the Creator. Pirkei Avot, a book of the Mishnah, teaches "Be as meticulous in performing a 'minor' mitzvah as you are with a 'major' one, because you don't know what kind of reward you'll get for various mitzvot." It also says, "Run after the most 'minor' mitzvah as you would after the most 'important' and flee from transgression, because doing one mitzvah draws you into doing another, and doing one transgression draws you into doing another, and because the reward for a mitzvah is a mitzvah and the punishment for a transgression is a transgression." In other words, every mitzvah is important, because even the most seemingly trivial mitzvot draw you into a pattern of leading your life in accordance with the Creator's wishes, rather than in accordance with your own.

But what about the so-called "Ten Commandments," the words recorded in Exodus 20, the words that the Creator personally wrote on the two stone tablets that Moses brought down from Mount Sinai (Ex. 31:18), which Moses smashed upon seeing the idolatry of the golden calf (Ex. 32:19)? In the Torah, these words are never referred to as the Ten Commandments. In the Torah, they are called Aseret ha-D'varim (Ex. 34:28, Deut. 4:13 and Deut. 10:4). In rabbinical texts, they are referred to as Aseret ha-Dibrot. The words d'varim and dibrot come from the Hebrew root Dalet-Beit-Reish, meaning word, speak or thing; thus, the phrase is accurately translated as the Ten Sayings, the Ten Statements, the Ten Declarations, the Ten Words or even the Ten Things, but not as the Ten Commandments, which would be Aseret ha-Mitzvot.

The Aseret ha-Dibrot are not understood as individual mitzvot; rather, they are categories or classifications of mitzvot. Each of the 613 mitzvot can be subsumed under one of these ten categories, some in more obvious ways than others.   For example, the mitzvah not to work on Shabbat rather obviously falls within the category of remembering the Sabbath day and keeping it holy. The mitzvah to fast on Yom Kippur fits into that category somewhat less obviously: all holidays are in some sense a Sabbath, and the category encompasses any mitzvah related to sacred time. The mitzvah not to stand aside while a person's life is in danger fits somewhat obviously into the category against murder. It is not particularly obvious, however, that the mitzvah not to embarrass a person fits within the category against murder: it causes the blood to drain from your face thereby shedding blood.

List of the Aseret ha–Dibrot

According to Judaism, the Aseret ha-Dibrot identify the following ten categories of mitzvot.   Other religions divide this passage differently. See The "Ten Commandments" Controversy below. Please remember that these are categories of the 613 mitzvot, which according to Jewish tradition are binding only upon Jews. The only mitzvot binding upon gentiles are the seven Noahic commandments. [5]
...

A Christian — Roman Catholic View

Called also simply THE COMMANDMENTS, COMMANDMENTS OF GOD, or THE DECALOGUE (Gr. deka, ten, and logos, a word), the Ten Words of Sayings, the latter name generally applied by the Greek Fathers.

The Ten Commandments are precepts bearing on

---

[5]Aseret ha-Dibrot: The Ten Commandments, Judaism 101, accessed 16 Dec 2024, https://www.jewfaq.org/10_commandments

the fundamental obligations of religion and morality and embodying the revealed expression of the Creator's will in relation to man's whole duty to God and to his fellow-creatures. They are found twice recorded in the Pentateuch, in Exodus 20 and Deuteronomy 5, but are given in an abridged form in the catechisms. Written by the finger of God on two tables of stone, this Divine code was received from the Almighty by Moses amid the thunders of Mount Sinai, and by him made the ground-work of the Mosaic Law. Christ resumed these Commandments in the double precept of charity--love of God and of the neighbour; He proclaimed them as binding under the New Law in Matthew 19 and in the Sermon on the Mount (Matthew 5). He also simplified or interpreted them, e.g. by declaring unnecessary oaths equally unlawful with false, by condemning hatred and calumny as well as murder, by enjoining even love of enemies, and by condemning indulgence of evil desires as fraught with the same malice as adultery (Matthew 5). The Church, on the other hand, after changing the day of rest from the Jewish Sabbath, or seventh day of the week, to the first, made the Third Commandment refer to Sunday as the day to be kept holy as the Lord's Day. The Council of Trent (Sess. VI, can. xix) condemns those who deny that the Ten Commandments are binding on Christians. ...[6]

Key Points From The Jewish View:

According to Jewish tradition, G-d gave the Jewish people 613 mitzvot (commandments).

...

But what about the so-called "Ten Commandments," the words recorded in Exodus

---

[6]Kevin Knight, 'The Ten Commandments', New Advent, accessed 16 Dec 2024, https://www.newadvent.org/cathen/04153a.htm.

20, the words that the Creator personally wrote on the two stone tablets that Moses brought down from Mount Sinai (Ex. 31:18), which Moses smashed upon seeing the idolatry of the golden calf (Ex. 32:19)? In the Torah, these words are never referred to as the Ten Commandments. In the Torah, they are called Aseret ha-D'varim (Ex. 34:28, Deut. 4:13 and Deut. 10:4). In rabbinical texts, they are referred to as Aseret ha-Dibrot.

...

Please remember that these are categories of the 613 mitzvot, which according to Jewish tradition are binding only upon Jews. The only mitzvot binding upon gentiles are the seven Noahic commandments. ...

My Comments On The Jewish–Talmudic View:

The Jewish quote emphasizes the preeminence of the **613 mitzvot (commandments).** **The 613 mitzvot is a rabbinic invention!** Likewise, **the seven Noahic commandments for gentiles is also a rabbinic innovation!**

The following is a very important text in the Jewish Scriptures regarding **the place of gentiles who sojourn among Israel:**

יב **מח** וְכִי־יָגוּר אִתְּךָ גֵּר וְעָשָׂה פֶסַח לַיהוָה הִמּוֹל לוֹ כָל־זָכָר וְאָז יִקְרַב לַעֲשֹׂתוֹ וְהָיָה כְּאֶזְרַח הָאָרֶץ וְכָל־עָרֵל לֹא־יֹאכַל בּוֹ:

12 48 And when a stranger shall sojourn with thee, and will keep the passover to Yehovah, let all his males be circumcised, and then let him come near and keep it; and he shall be as one that is born in the land; but no uncircumcised person shall eat thereof.

מט	תּוֹרָ֣ה אַחַ֔ת יִהְיֶ֖ה לָֽאֶזְרָ֑ח וְלַגֵּ֖ר הַגָּ֥ר
בְּתוֹכְכֶֽם׃

<u>49</u> One Torah shall be to him that is homeborn, and unto the stranger that sojourneth among you.'

נ	וַיַּֽעֲשׂ֖וּ כָּל־בְּנֵ֣י יִשְׂרָאֵ֑ל כַּאֲשֶׁ֨ר צִוָּ֤ה יְהֹוָה֙
אֶת־מֹשֶׁ֣ה וְאֶֽת־אַהֲרֹ֔ן כֵּ֖ן עָשֽׂוּ׃

<u>50</u> Thus did all the children of Israel; as Yehovah commanded Moses and Aaron, so did they.

נא	וַיְהִ֕י בְּעֶ֖צֶם הַיּ֣וֹם הַזֶּ֑ה הוֹצִ֨יא יְהֹוָ֜ה אֶת־בְּנֵ֤י
יִשְׂרָאֵל֙ מֵאֶ֣רֶץ מִצְרַ֔יִם עַל־צִבְאֹתָֽם׃

<u>51</u> And it came to pass the selfsame day that Yehovah did bring the children of Israel out of the land of Egypt by their hosts.

[Exodus 12:48-51 The Pill Tanakh]

12 <u>49</u> One Torah shall be to him that is homeborn, and unto the stranger that sojourneth among you.

[Exodus 12:49 The Pill Tanakh]

Thus, the Jewish Scriptures are in opposition to the non–Biblically based teachings of man, including Talmudists! The Scriptures clearly show that both Jews and gentiles are to follow one Torah. There are not a separate set of 613 laws for Jews and 7 Noahic laws for gentiles! **There is just ONE GOD — AND ONE TORAH!**

Key Points From The Roman Catholic View:

The Church, on the other hand, after changing the day of rest from the Jewish Sabbath, or

seventh day of the week, to the first, made the Third Commandment refer to Sunday as the day to be kept holy as the Lord's Day. The Council of Trent (Sess. VI, can. xix) condemns those who deny that the Ten Commandments are binding on Christians. ...

My Comments On The Roman Catholic View:

Just like the Jewish Talmudists, the Roman Catholic church appears to quote Scripture as a matter of expediency . Many of their tenets and doctrines also derive from extra–Biblical, man–made customs, edicts and laws!

Changing the Sabbath is a direct breach of the fourth (4th) of the 'Ten Commandments' in the Jewish Scriptures. Notwithstanding, the Catholic quote includes the statement, *"The Council of Trent (Sess. VI, can. xix) condemns those who deny that the Ten Commandments are binding on Christians."*

Yet, I would be remiss if I failed to mention the Roman Catholic de facto response to the second (2nd) commandment as recorded in the Hebrew–language based Masoretic text.

Although Catholic Bibles record the commandment related to idols, beginning with *"Thou shalt have no other gods before Me. Thou shalt not make unto thee a graven image, ..."* in practice they disparage that commandment by not only allowing images (idols) in their homes and houses of worship but also commonly directing their prayers to them!

In looking for articles regarding a Roman Catholic understanding of the second commandment regarding idols, I came across the following, which I have taken a portion of:

It is right to warn people against the sin of idolatry when they are committing it. But calling Catholics idolaters because they have images of Christ and the saints is based on misunderstanding or ignorance of what the Bible says about the purpose and uses (both good and bad) of statues.

Anti-Catholic writer Loraine Boettner, in his book *Roman Catholicism,* makes the blanket statement, "God has forbidden the use of images in worship" (281). Yet if people were to "search the scriptures" (John 5:39), they would find the opposite is true. God forbade the worship of statues, but he did not forbid the religious use of statues. Instead, he actually commanded their use in religious contexts!

God Said to Make Them

People who oppose religious statuary forget about the many passages where the Lord commands the making of statues. For example: "And you shall make two cherubim of gold [i.e., two gold statues of angels]; of hammered work shall you make them, on the two ends of the mercy seat. Make one cherub on the one end, and one cherub on the other end; of one piece of the mercy seat shall you make the cherubim on its two ends. The cherubim shall spread out their wings above, overshadowing the mercy seat with their wings, their faces one to another; toward the mercy seat shall the faces of the cherubim be" (Ex. 25:18–20).

David gave Solomon the plan "for the altar of incense made of refined gold, and its weight; also his plan for the golden chariot of the cherubim that spread their wings and covered the ark of the covenant of the Lord. All this he made clear by the writing of the hand of the Lord concerning it all" (1 Chr. 28:18–19). David's plan for the temple included statues of angels.

Similarly Ezekiel 41:17-18 describes graven (carved) images in the idealized temple he was shown in a vision, for he writes, "On the walls round about in the inner room and [on] the nave were carved likenesses of cherubim."[7]

In my opinion, it is a fault of human relativism which brings about such defenses of worship practices as spoken above. It is one thing to associate direct commands given by יְהֹוָה Yehovah for purposes of *His* worship with teachings of the Roman Catholic church unrelated to direct commands of יְהֹוָה Yehovah!

The recorded accounts of the Jewish Scriptures are violated by such expressions of worship unrelated to the direct commands of יְהֹוָה Yehovah to *His* people Israel!

It is, perhaps, a subtle distinction, but equating commands given by the Creator of the Universe for purposes of *His* own direct worship **with the pagan practices of the Roman Catholic church is an absolute abomination and assault on** *The Word of God* as directed to the Israelite (Jewish) people!

Obviously, The Ten Commandments hold a special place for Jews as well as Christians, regardless of their motivation!

In this chapter, I addressed the issue of just what is considered to be Biblical Judaism.

I discussed Karaite Judaism as the better representation of just what Biblical Judaism is — following the Hebrew–language based Jewish Scriptures in Halakha (how we walk), understand and observe our faith.

In looking at core principles, I presented views on The Ten Commandments from a Jewish viewpoint followed by a Roman Catholic view.

In the next chapter, I present The Ten Commandments, separating the verses with snippets from the Leningrad Codex next to font based Hebrew of the same text, along with English translations.

---

[7]Robert H. Brom, 'Do Catholics Worship Statues?', Catholic Answers, accessed 22 Dec 2024, https://www.catholic.com/tract/do-catholics-worship-statues.

The Crown Of The Torah

The Ten Commandments

עֲשֶׂרֶת הַדְּבָרִים

The Ten Commandments

The Ten Commandments in the Leningrad Codex
(right column, top, first six verses, page 91 in pdf)
Exodus 20:10b - 12

עֲשֶׂרֶת הַדְּבָרִים

The Ten Commandments

The Ten Commandments in the Leningrad Codex
(middle-column, middle to left-column-bottom, page 90 in pdf)
Exodus 20:1 - 10a

Exodus 20:1-12

The 10 Commandments In The Leningrad Codex

These are the words written by the Finger of Yehovah on the two tablets of stone, which He commanded Moses to place into the Ark of the Testimony (אֲרוֹן הָעֵדֻת), also known as the Ark of the Covenant (אֲרוֹן בְּרִית־יְהֹוָה)!

אֲ וַיְדַבֵּר אֱלֹהִים אֵת כָּל־הַדְּבָרִים הָאֵלֶּה לֵאמֹר: בֲ אָנֹכִי יהוה אֱלֹהֶיךָ אֲשֶׁר הוֹצֵאתִיךָ מֵאֶרֶץ מִצְרַיִם מִבֵּית עֲבָדִים

1. And God spoke all these words, saying: 2. I am Yehovah thy God, who brought thee out of the land of Egypt, out of the house of bondage.

גֹ לֹא יִהְיֶה־לְךָ֩ אֱלֹהִ֨ים
אֲחֵרִ֖ים עַל־פָּנָ֑י לֹא
תַעֲשֶׂה־לְךָ֣ פֶ֫סֶל֙ ׀
וְכָל־תְּמוּנָ֡ה אֲשֶׁ֣ר
בַּשָּׁמַ֣יִם֙ ׀ מִמַּ֡עַל וַֽאֲשֶׁ֣ר
בָּאָ֖רֶץ מִתָּ֑חַת וַֽאֲשֶׁ֣ר
בַּמַּ֖יִם ׀ מִתַּ֣חַת לָאָ֑רֶץ
לֹא־תִשְׁתַּחֲוֶ֣ה לָהֶם֒
וְלֹא תָעָבְדֵ֑ם כִּ֣י אָנֹכִ֞י
יְהֹוָ֤ה אֱלֹהֶ֨יךָ֙ אֵ֣ל
קַנָּ֔א פֹּקֵ֞ד עֲוֹ֤ן אָבֹ֨ת
עַל־בָּנִ֖ים עַל־שִׁלֵּשִׁ֑ים
וְעַל־רִבֵּעִ֖ים לְשֹׂנְאָֽי׃
דֹ וְעֹ֤שֶׂה חֶ֨סֶד֙ לַאֲלָפִ֔ים
לְאֹהֲבַ֖י וּלְשֹׁמְרֵ֥י מִצְוֹתָֽי׃

3. Thou shalt have no other gods before Me. Thou shalt not make unto thee a graven image, nor any manner of likeness, of any thing that is in heaven above, or that is in the earth beneath, or that is in the water under the earth; thou shalt not bow down unto them, nor serve them; for I Yehovah thy God am a jealous God, visiting the iniquity of the fathers upon the children unto the third and fourth generation of them that hate Me; 4. and showing mercy unto the thousandth generation of them that love Me and keep My commandments.

ה   לֹא   תִשָּׂא
אֶת־שֵׁם־יְהוָה אֱלֹהֶיךָ
לַשָּׁוְא   כִּי   לֹא   יְנַקֶּה
יְהוָה   אֵת   אֲשֶׁר־יִשָּׂא
אֶת־שְׁמוֹ לַשָּׁוְא:

5. Thou shalt not lift up the Name of Yehovah thy God as to declare Him worthless; for Yehovah will not hold him guiltless who takes His Name falsely.

ו   זָכוֹר   אֶת־יוֹם   הַשַּׁבָּת
לְקַדְּשׁוֹ
שֵׁשֶׁת יָמִים תַּעֲבֹד וְעָשִׂיתָ
כָל־מְלַאכְתֶּךָ וְיוֹם הַשְּׁבִיעִי
שַׁבָּת ׀ לַיהוָה אֱלֹהֶיךָ לֹא־
תַעֲשֶׂה כָל־מְלָאכָה אַתָּה ׀
וּבִנְךָ־וּבִתֶּךָ עַבְדְּךָ וַאֲמָתְךָ
וּבְהֶמְתֶּךָ   וְגֵרְךָ   אֲשֶׁר
בִּשְׁעָרֶיךָ
כִּי שֵׁשֶׁת־יָמִים עָשָׂה יְהוָה
אֶת־הַשָּׁמַיִם וְאֶת־הָאָרֶץ
אֶת־הַיָּם וְאֶת־כָּל־אֲשֶׁר־בָּם
וַיָּנַח בַּיּוֹם הַשְּׁבִיעִי עַל־כֵּן
בֵּרַךְ יְהוָה אֶת־יוֹם הַשַּׁבָּת
וַיְקַדְּשֵׁהוּ:

6. Remember the sabbath day, to keep it holy. Six days shalt thou labour, and do all thy work; but the seventh day is a sabbath unto

Yehovah thy God, in it thou shalt not do any manner of work, thou, nor thy son, nor thy daughter, nor thy man-servant, nor thy maid-servant, nor thy cattle, nor thy stranger that is within thy gates; for in six days Yehovah made heaven and earth, the sea, and all that in them is, and rested on the seventh day; wherefore Yehovah blessed the sabbath day, and hallowed it.

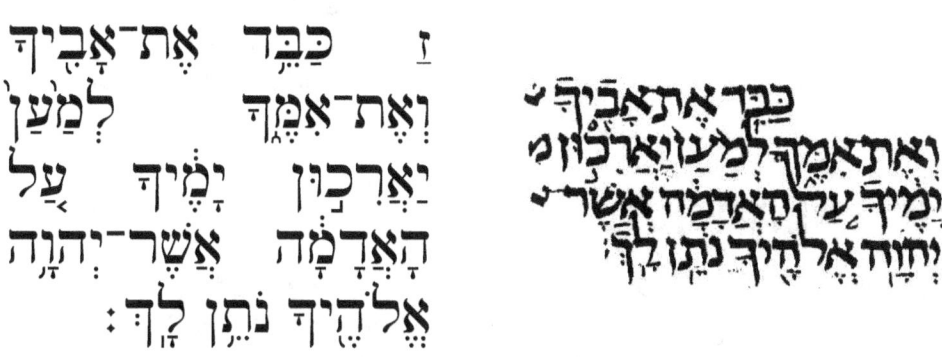

7. Honour thy father and thy mother, that thy days may be long upon the land which Yehovah thy God giveth thee.

8. Thou shalt not murder.

9. Thou shalt commit adultery.

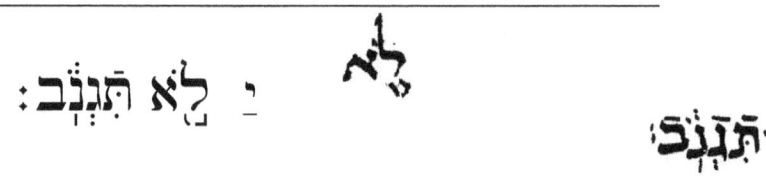

10. Thou shalt not steal.

יא לֹא־תַעֲנֶה בְרֵעֲךָ
עֵד שָׁקֶר׃

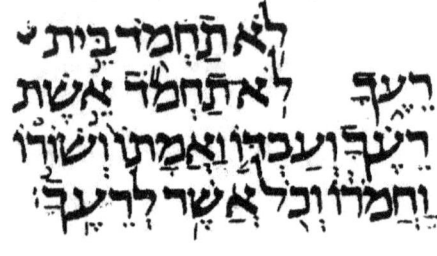

11. Thou shalt not bear false witness against thy neighbour.
Literally: 'Thou shalt not answer a person to whom you are
associated with a witness/testimony that is a lie, deceitful, false.'

יב לֹא תַחְמֹד בֵּית
רֵעֲךָ לֹא־תַחְמֹד אֵשֶׁת
רֵעֲךָ וְעַבְדּוֹ וַאֲמָתוֹ
וְשׁוֹרוֹ וַחֲמֹרוֹ וְכֹל
אֲשֶׁר לְרֵעֲךָ׃

12. Thou shalt not covet thy neighbour's house; thou shalt not covet
thy neighbour's wife, nor his man-servant, nor his maid-servant, nor
his ox, nor his ass, nor any thing that is thy neighbour's.

עֲשֶׂרֶת הַדְּבָרִים — The Ten Commandments

יְהוָה [Yehovah] considered that the two tablets of stone, on which He personally wrote the Ten Commandments, were of such importance that He commanded Moses to make a box of acacia wood and place them into it.

That box of acacia wood is better known as the Ark of the Covenant (אֲרֹון בְּרִית־יְהוָה)!

Thus, the place where the "written by the finger of אֱלֹהִים [Elohim]" Ten Commandments were located was known among the ancient Israelites as the earthly dwelling place of the Creator of the Universe!

If יְהוָה [Yehovah] held His Ten Commandments to be in such esteem, is it too much a stretch to think that we should hold them in the highest regard ourselves?

Might we consider that, in studying them, we may come to learn to comprehend that our own reason for being could be discerned by knowing the אֱלֹהִים [Elohim] (God) of אַבְרָהָם Abraham, יִצְחָק Isaac and יַעֲקֹב Jacob personally?

It is with these sentiments that I invite you to join the many who have found delight in the reading of the words of יְהוָה [Yehovah] and who desire to live by them.

In the original **Leningrad Codex, the Masoretes** marked the end of most verses with a **Sof Pasuq,** a Cantillation mark which looks like a colon (:). Another mark, **Silluq**, a small vertical line to the left of the vowel with the word's main accent, *is found in the last word of every verse in the Hebrew Scriptures!*

In Exodus 20, above, where, to the side of each Hebrew font-based verse I show the image from the corresponding verse in the photo-facsimile* **Leningrad Codex,** I believe that I have correctly captured those verses just as they appear in the actual **Leningrad Codex** itself *(* the "pdf" is referred to as a **"photo–facsimile"** since it is a **"photographic copy"** of the original Leningrad Codex).*

For some images of verses, which actually break over different columns in the three columns of the original, I have placed the image parts next to each other in an effort to make them appear more natural.

עֲשֶׂרֶת הַדְּבָרִים — "The Ten Declarations"

In the Torah, only three verses mention the term for what is commonly known as **The Ten Commandments.**   Those verses are Exodus 34:28, Deuteronomy 4:13, 10:4.   However, the word most often translated as "Commandments" is **NOT** from the Hebrew root **צֻו, הצֻוה** (tzav, tz'vah = command, order)! Rather, in the phrase **עֲשֶׂרֶת הַדְּבָרִים** (aseret ha-devarim), **עֲשֶׂרֶת** (aseret) means the number ten (10), while **דְּבָרִים** (devarim) often translated as "words" or "things," is better translated as "statements" or "declarations!"   Thus, **עֲשֶׂרֶת הַדְּבָרִים** **(= The Ten Statements/Declarations).**

In the **Masoretic text,** aka *The Leningrad Codex,* there are <u>12 verses</u> for the complete "Ten Commandments!"   Verses 1 and 2 go together for the 1st "commandment" and verses 3 and 4 go together for the 2nd "commandment." **The rest of the verses are all standalone, to complete the whole, for a total of <u>10 commandments</u> (statements/declarations).**

Other Jewish Hebrew-English publications use <u>**14 verses**</u> for the Ten Commandments.   They break up the 2nd and 4th commandments (verses 3 and 6 respectively, herein) into multiple verses and combine the three verses, *'Thou Shalt Not Kill, Commit Adultery and Steal'* into <u>one single verse</u>!

Christian Bibles use <u>**17 verses**</u> for the Ten Commandments, adding even more breaks to the text!   **No other publications, that I am aware of, honor the sublime rendering of The Ten Commandments found in the Leningrad Codex!**   Please, be advised that these are the same verses written on stone tablets "by the finger of Yehovah," which He commanded Moses to place into the Ark of the Covenant!

It is my hope that all who view this presentation of the 10 Commandments of Exodus 20 will be able to discern that the *Masoretes* fully intended each hand–written verse to be separated at the *Silluq/Sof-Pasuq,* while so many *"moderns"* have chosen to represent the Hebrew and English texts incorrectly!   This includes Jewish and Christian publications as well as the Westminster Leningrad Codex (WLC - www.tanach.us), which is the electronic source of which I had used my copyrighted C++ Library to write C++ code to convert from a Multi–wide UTF–16 Unicode format (not editable) to my copyrighted ASCII based UTF–8 web–font format (editable).

Further, it is my sincere desire that יְהֹוָה * **[Yehovah] is honored, glorified and exalted** in this present work, including the whole of *The-Iconoclast.org online Westminster Leningrad Codex based Hebrew, JPS 1917 based English Scriptures and my self–published book, The Pill Tanakh: Hebrew–English Jewish Scriptures* (in Three volumes: Torah, Neviim–Prophets, Ketuvim–Writings).

* יְהֹוָה **[Yehovah] is the Name of God in Hebrew.**

יְהֹוָה [Yehovah] means:

הָיָה [Hayah] He who was,

הֹוֶה [Hoveh] He who is,

יִהְיֶה [Yihyeh] He who will be.

Seek Yehovah

נה וּ דִּרְשׁוּ יְהֹוָה בְּהִמָּצְאוֹ קְרָאֻהוּ בִּהְיוֹתוֹ
קָרוֹב:

55 <u>6</u> Seek ye Yehovah while He may be found, call ye upon Him while He is near;

ז יַעֲזֹב רָשָׁע דַּרְכּוֹ וְאִישׁ אָוֶן מַחְשְׁבֹתָיו וְיָשֹׁב
אֶל־יְהֹוָה וִירַחֲמֵהוּ וְאֶל־אֱלֹהֵינוּ כִּי־יַרְבֶּה
לִסְלוֹחַ:

<u>7</u> Let the wicked forsake his way, and the man of iniquity his thoughts; and let him return unto Yehovah, and He will have compassion upon him, and to our God, for He will abundantly pardon.

ח כִּי לֹא מַחְשְׁבוֹתַי מַחְשְׁבוֹתֵיכֶם וְלֹא דַרְכֵיכֶם
דְּרָכָי נְאֻם יְהֹוָה:

<u>8</u> For My thoughts are not your thoughts, neither are your ways My ways, saith Yehovah.

ט כִּי־גָבְהוּ שָׁמַיִם מֵאָרֶץ כֵּן גָּבְהוּ דְרָכַי
מִדַּרְכֵיכֶם וּמַחְשְׁבֹתַי מִמַּחְשְׁבֹתֵיכֶם:

<u>9</u> For as the heavens are higher than the earth, so are My ways higher than your ways, and My thoughts than your thoughts.
[Isaiah 55:6-9 The Pill Tanakh]

55 <u>6</u> **Seek ye Yehovah while He may be found, call ye upon Him while He is near;**

<u>7</u> **Let the wicked forsake his way, and**

the man of iniquity his thoughts; and let him return unto Yehovah, and He will have compassion upon him, and to our God, for He will abundantly pardon.
[Isaiah 55:6-7 The Pill Tanakh]

Repentance. In the Biblical sense, as in Isaiah 55:7,

repenting means וְיָשֹׁב אֶל־יְהוָה **and let him return to Yehovah.**

But what is **'returning to Yehovah?'**

ג ה בְּטַח אֶל־יְהוָה בְּכָל־לִבֶּךָ וְאֶל־בִּינָתְךָ אַל־תִּשָּׁעֵן׃

3 5 Trust in Yehovah with all thy heart, and lean not upon thine own understanding.

ו בְּכָל־דְּרָכֶיךָ דָעֵהוּ וְהוּא יְיַשֵּׁר אֹרְחֹתֶיךָ׃

6 In all thy ways acknowledge Him, and He will direct thy paths.

ז אַל־תְּהִי חָכָם בְּעֵינֶיךָ יְרָא אֶת־יְהוָה וְסוּר מֵרָע׃

7 Be not wise in thine own eyes; fear Yehovah, and depart from evil;

יג אַשְׁרֵי אָדָם מָצָא חָכְמָה וְאָדָם יָפִיק תְּבוּנָה׃

13 Happy is the man that findeth wisdom, and the man that obtaineth understanding.

יד כִּי טוֹב סַחְרָהּ מִסְּחַר־כָּסֶף וּמֵחָרוּץ תְּבוּאָתָהּ׃

<u>14</u> For the merchandise of it is better than the merchandise of silver, and the gain thereof than fine gold.

יַה   יְקָרָה הִיא מִפְּנִינִים וְכָל־חֲפָצֶיךָ לָא
יִשְׁווּ־בָהּ:

<u>15</u> She is more precious than rubies; and all the things thou canst desire are not to be compared unto her.

יַו אֹרֶךְ יָמִים בִּימִינָהּ בִּשְׂמֹאולָהּ עֹשֶׁר וְכָבוֹד:

<u>16</u> Length of days is in her right hand; in her left hand are riches and honour.

יַז דְּרָכֶיהָ דַרְכֵי־נֹעַם וְכָל־נְתִיבוֹתֶיהָ שָׁלוֹם:

<u>17</u> Her ways are ways of pleasantness, and all her paths are peace.

יַח עֵץ־חַיִּים הִיא לַמַּחֲזִיקִים בָּהּ וְתֹמְכֶיהָ מְאֻשָּׁר:

<u>18</u> She is a tree of life to them that lay hold upon her, and happy is every one that holdest her fast.
[Proverbs 3:5-7, 13-18 The Pill Tanakh]

You can see that I have used passages from Scripture to reinforce points I have wanted to express. Proverbs 3:5 certainly sets the requirement of repentance succinctly!

3 <u>5</u> Trust in Yehovah with all thy heart, and lean not upon thine own understanding. [Proverbs 3:5 The Pill Tanakh]

Can anyone come into a personal relationship with יְהוָה Yehovah _without_ _repenting_ _first_, _with_ _humility_?

ו ח הִגִּיד לְךָ אָדָם מַה־טֶּוֹב וּמָה־יְהֹוָה דּוֹרֵשׁ
מִמְּךָ כִּי אִם־עֲשֶׂוֹת מִשְׁפָּט וְאַהֲבַת חֶסֶד וְהַצְנֵעַ
לֶכֶת עִם־אֱלֹהֶיךָ:

6 8 It hath been told thee, O man, what is good, and what Yehovah doth require of thee: only to do justly, and to love mercy, and to walk humbly with thy God. [Micah 6:8 The Pill Tanakh]

ב ג בַּקְּשׁוּ אֶת־יְהֹוָה כָּל־עַנְוֵי הָאָרֶץ אֲשֶׁר מִשְׁפָּטוֹ
פָּעָלוּ בַּקְּשׁוּ־צֶדֶק בַּקְּשׁוּ עֲנָוָה אוּלַי תִּסָּתְרוּ בְּיוֹם
אַף־יְהֹוָה:

2 3 Seek ye Yehovah, all ye humble of the earth, that have executed His ordinance; seek righteousness, seek humility. It may be ye shall be hid in the day of Yehovah's anger. [Zephaniah 2:3 The Pill Tanakh]

Obviously, anyone who was raised in a family with even a modicum of religious upbringing will have a knowledge of "God." The three major world religions of Judaism, Christianity and Islam will have contributed to that understanding. Certainly, that does not mean that those persons have a meaningful relationship with the Almighty, but perhaps nothing more than a general knowledge.

Of course, each of those religious systems provide methodologies for greater faith, such as a devotion to study or even having a discipline of saying certain prayers, wearing religious attire, etc.

No doubt there are some people who have an understanding of God after experiencing some sort of encounter that changes their life. That experience may be "supernatural" like the people of Israel in Elijah's day, who, after seeing the sacrifice on an altar soaked with water saw it totally consumed by the fire of Yehovah (1 Kings 18)! They said, **'Yehovah, He is God; Yehovah, He is God.'**

יח לח וַתִּפֹּל אֵשׁ־יְהוָֹה וַתֹּאכַל אֶת־הָעֹלָה
וְאֶת־הָעֵצִים וְאֶת־הָאֲבָנִים וְאֶת־הֶעָפָר
וְאֶת־הַמַּיִם אֲשֶׁר־בַּתְּעָלָה לִחֵכָה:

18 38 Then the fire of Yehovah fell, and consumed the burnt-offering, and the wood, and the stones, and the dust, and licked up the water that was in the trench.

לט וַיַּרְא כָּל־הָעָם וַיִּפְּלוּ עַל־פְּנֵיהֶם וַיֹּאמְרוּ
יְהוָֹה הוּא הָאֱלֹהִים יְהוָֹה הוּא הָאֱלֹהִים:

39 And when all the people saw it, they fell on their faces; and they said: 'Yehovah, He is God; Yehovah, He is God.'
[1 Kings 18:38–39 The Pill Tanakh]

Having had any experience which helps to turn or return one to acknowledgement and trust in יְהוָֹה Yehovah is no doubt a good place to start one's continued journey in this life!

I said, **turn** or **return to** יְהוָֹה Yehovah as I know some folks have never had a relationship with the Almighty God, although many believe they have had such in the past.

For those who have been influenced by Christian doctrine (as in the Western world of our day), as I understand them, so many have concluded that they have nothing to **repent of,** perhaps because in professing *Jesus* they have come to believe that their past, present and future sins continue to be atoned for by Jesus!

Moreover, **if they do not repent and do not live by the clear instructions of the written Torah of** יְהוָֹה **Yehovah, then at the judgment when they come into the presence of the Almighty God will they be able to stand?** By their attitudes, many believe so! It appears that they believe that they don't have to do anything over and above what they currently do in order to come into the presence of Almighty God!

I believe it is unfortunate that **their doctrine puts a greater emphasis on <u>how</u> <u>one</u> <u>thinks</u> rather than on how one acts!**

Regardless of one's religious background, **the written Torah** (also known as the first five books in the Hebrew–language based Jewish Scriptures) **itself provides answers to having a sincere relationship with the Almighty God.**

30 <u>11</u> For this commandment which I command thee this day, it is not too hard for thee, neither is it far off. [Deuteronomy 30:11 The Pill Tanakh]

לֹ יֵּא כִּי הַמִּצְוָה הַזֹּאת אֲשֶׁר אָנֹכִי מְצַוְּךָ הַיָּוֹם לֹא־נִפְלֵאת הִוא מִמְּךָ וְלֹא רְחֹקָה הִוא׃

30 <u>11</u> For this commandment which I command thee this day, it is not too hard for thee, neither is it far off.

יֵּב לֹא בַשָּׁמַיִם הִוא לֵאמֹר מִי יַעֲלֶה־לָּנוּ הַשָּׁמַיְמָה וְיִקָּחֶהָ לָּנוּ וְיַשְׁמִעֵנוּ אֹתָהּ וְנַעֲשֶׂנָּה׃

<u>12</u> It is not in heaven, that thou shouldest say: 'Who shall go up for us to heaven, and bring it unto us, and make us to hear it, that we may do it?'

יֵּג וְלֹא־מֵעֵבֶר לַיָּם הִוא לֵאמֹר מִי יַעֲבָר־לָּנוּ אֶל־עֵבֶר הַיָּם וְיִקָּחֶהָ לָּנוּ וְיַשְׁמִעֵנוּ אֹתָהּ וְנַעֲשֶׂנָּה׃

<u>13</u> Neither is it beyond the sea, that thou shouldest say: 'Who shall go over the sea for us, and bring it unto us, and make us to hear it, that we may do it?'

יֵּד כִּי־קָרוֹב אֵלֶיךָ הַדָּבָר מְאֹד בְּפִיךָ וּבִלְבָבְךָ לַעֲשֹׂתוֹ׃

<u>14</u> But the word is very nigh unto thee, in thy mouth, and in thy heart, that thou mayest do it.

יֵּה רְאֵה נָתַתִּי לְפָנֶיךָ הַיּוֹם אֶת־הַחַיִּים וְאֶת־הַטּוֹב וְאֶת־הַמָּוֶת וְאֶת־הָרָע׃

15 See, I have set before thee this day life and good, and death and evil,

יה אֲשֶׁ֨ר אָנֹכִ֣י מְצַוְּךָ֮ הַיּוֹם֒ לְאַֽהֲבָ֞ה אֶת־יְהוָ֣ה אֱלֹהֶ֗יךָ לָלֶ֤כֶת בִּדְרָכָיו֙ וְלִשְׁמֹ֞ר מִצְוֺתָ֧יו וְחֻקֹּתָ֛יו וּמִשְׁפָּטָ֖יו וְחָיִ֣יתָ וְרָבִ֑יתָ וּבֵֽרַכְךָ֙ יְהוָ֣ה אֱלֹהֶ֔יךָ בָּאָ֕רֶץ אֲשֶׁר־אַתָּ֥ה בָא־שָׁ֖מָּה לְרִשְׁתָּֽהּ׃

16 in that I command thee this day to love Yehovah thy God, to walk in His ways, and to keep His commandments and His statutes and His ordinances; then thou shalt live and multiply, and Yehovah thy God shall bless thee in the land whither thou goest in to possess it.

יז וְאִם־יִפְנֶ֥ה לְבָבְךָ֖ וְלֹ֣א תִשְׁמָ֑ע וְנִדַּחְתָּ֗ וְהִֽשְׁתַּחֲוִ֛יתָ לֵֽאלֹהִ֥ים אֲחֵרִ֖ים וַעֲבַדְתָּֽם׃

17 But if thy heart turn away, and thou wilt not hear, but shalt be drawn away, and worship other gods, and serve them;

יח הִגַּ֤דְתִּי לָכֶם֙ הַיּ֔וֹם כִּ֥י אָבֹ֖ד תֹּאבֵד֑וּן לֹא־תַאֲרִיכֻ֤ן יָמִים֙ עַל־הָ֣אֲדָמָ֔ה אֲשֶׁ֨ר אַתָּ֜ה עֹבֵ֧ר אֶת־הַיַּרְדֵּ֛ן לָבֹ֥א שָׁ֖מָּה לְרִשְׁתָּֽהּ׃

18 I declare unto you this day, that ye shall surely perish; ye shall not prolong your days upon the land, whither thou passest over the Jordan to go in to possess it.

יט הַעִדֹ֨תִי בָכֶ֜ם הַיּ֗וֹם אֶת־הַשָּׁמַ֙יִם֙ וְאֶת־הָאָ֔רֶץ הַחַיִּ֤ים וְהַמָּ֙וֶת֙ נָתַ֣תִּי לְפָנֶ֔יךָ הַבְּרָכָ֖ה וְהַקְּלָלָ֑ה וּבָֽחַרְתָּ֙ בַּֽחַיִּ֔ים לְמַ֥עַן תִּֽחְיֶ֖ה אַתָּ֥ה וְזַרְעֶֽךָ׃

19 I call heaven and earth to witness against you this day, that I have set before thee life and death, the blessing and the curse; therefore choose life, that thou mayest live, thou and thy seed;

כ לְאַהֲבָה֙ אֶת־יְהוָ֣ה אֱלֹהֶ֔יךָ לִשְׁמֹ֥עַ בְּקֹל֖וֹ וּלְדָבְקָה־ב֑וֹ
כִּ֣י ה֤וּא חַיֶּ֙יךָ֙ וְאֹ֣רֶךְ יָמֶ֔יךָ לָשֶׁ֖בֶת עַל־הָ֣אֲדָמָ֔ה אֲשֶׁר֩ נִשְׁבַּ֨ע
יְהוָ֧ה לַאֲבֹתֶ֛יךָ לְאַבְרָהָ֥ם לְיִצְחָ֖ק וּֽלְיַעֲקֹ֑ב לָתֵ֥ת לָהֶֽם׃

<u>20</u> to love Yehovah thy God, to hearken to His voice,
and to cleave unto Him; for that is thy life, and the
length of thy days; that thou mayest dwell in the land
which Yehovah swore unto thy fathers, to Abraham,
to Isaac, and to Jacob, to give them.
[Deuteronomy 30:11–20 The Pill Tanakh]

ל יה רְאֵ֨ה נָתַ֤תִּי לְפָנֶ֙יךָ֙ הַיּ֔וֹם אֶת־הַֽחַיִּ֖ים
וְאֶת־הַטּ֑וֹב וְאֶת־הַמָּ֖וֶת וְאֶת־הָרָֽע׃

**30 15 See, I have set before thee this day
life and good, and death and evil,**

יו אֲשֶׁ֣ר אָנֹכִ֣י מְצַוְּךָ֮ הַיּוֹם֒ לְאַהֲבָ֞ה אֶת־יְהוָ֤ה
אֱלֹהֶ֙יךָ֙ לָלֶ֣כֶת בִּדְרָכָ֔יו וְלִשְׁמֹ֛ר מִצְוֺתָ֥יו וְחֻקֹּתָ֖יו
וּמִשְׁפָּטָ֑יו וְחָיִ֣יתָ וְרָבִ֔יתָ וּבֵרַכְךָ֙ יְהוָ֣ה אֱלֹהֶ֔יךָ
בָּאָ֕רֶץ אֲשֶׁר־אַתָּ֥ה בָא־שָׁ֖מָּה לְרִשְׁתָּֽהּ׃

**16 in that I command thee this day to love
Yehovah thy God, to walk in His ways,
<u>and</u> <u>to</u> <u>keep</u> <u>His</u> <u>commandments</u> <u>and</u> <u>His</u>
<u>statutes</u> <u>and</u> <u>His</u> <u>ordinances</u>; then thou
shalt live and multiply, and Yehovah thy
God shall bless thee in the land whither
thou goest in to possess it.**
[Deuteronomy 30:15–16 The Pill Tanakh]

**How does one come to know about the commandments,
statutes and ordinances which are supposed to be kept?** The
obvious answer, to me, is by a discipline of reading the Jewish
Scriptures on a regular basis!

I highly recommend for anyone who is interested in improving their relationship with the Almighty God to take on the <u>discipline</u> <u>of</u> <u>a</u> <u>Scripture</u> <u>reading</u> <u>plan</u> that will help provide a framework for you to read it in its entirety through each year. [1]

Moreover, for any of you who are not familiar with the ancient Hebrew language as found in the handwritten Leningrad Codex, I would encourage you to begin the process of learning to read and understand it!

גּ ט כִּי־אָז אֶהְפֹּךְ אֶל־עַמִּים שָׂפָה בְרוּרָה לִקְרֹא כֻלָּם בְּשֵׁם יְהֹוָה לְעָבְדוֹ שְׁכֶם אֶחָד:

3 9 For then will I turn to the peoples a pure language, that they may all call upon the name of Yehovah, to serve Him with one consent. [Zephaniah 3:9 The Pill Tanakh]

If you are unfamiliar with the Hebrew language, I am including a couple of charts which may introduce you to Hebrew! Below, please find the following charts, first the Hebrew letters, followed by vowel pointers and a brief introduction to Hebrew Cantillation. It is my hope that you come to recognize Hebrew letters and vowels as a starting place to facilitate a study of Biblical Hebrew!

---

[1] The following are two internet sources for reading the Scriptures daily throughout the year. Leningrad Codex Hebrew Modified JPS 1917 English Daily Readings, online at https://www.the-iconoclast.org/resources/daily/read_Tanakh.php.
Downloadable Pdf 'Read Scripture In–A–Year!' can be found online at http://sarshalom.us/resources/scripture/read_scripture-in-a-year.pdf.

HEBREW LETTERS

LETTER	NAME	PRONUNCIATION
א	Aleph	Orig. the glottal stop. Now silent in the middle of words if it has no vowel; otherwise it is pronounced according to the accompanying vowel sign.
בּ	Bet	**b**
ב	Vet	**bh, v**
גּ	Gimel	Pronounced like **g** in **get**
ג	Gimel	Orig. pronounced – with a slight aspiration of the sound – like **gh.**
דּ	Dalet	**d**
ד	Dalet	Orig. pronounced like **th** in **this.**
ה	He	**h**
ו	Vav	**v**
ז	Zayin	**z**
ח	Het	Pronounced like **ch** in Scot. **loch.** It is a guttural sound made in the back of the throat.
ט	Tet	An emphatic **t**
י	Yod	**y**

LETTER	NAME	PRONUNCIATION
כ	Kaph	k
ך	Kaph Sofit	k (at end of a word)
כ	Khaph	kh
ך	Khaph Sofit	kh (at end of a word)
ל	Lamed	l
מ	Mem	m
ם	Mem Sofit	m (at end of a word)
נ	Nun	n
ן	Nun Sofit	n (at end of a word)
ס	Samekh	s
ע	Ayin	A strong guttural sound, like a deep *aw.*
פ	Pe	p
פ	Phe	f
ף	Phe Sofit	f (at end of a word)
צ	Tzade	tz – Occasionally pronounced like an emphatic *s.*
ץ	Tzade Sofit	tz – Occasionally pronounced like an emphatic *s.*

LETTER	NAME	PRONUNCIATION
ק	Quf	an emphatic *k.*
ר	Resh	r (like a Spanish **rolled or trilled 'r'** (rolled with tongue). In the Hebrew the sound is made with a **rolling/trilling** vibration in back of the throat).
שׁ	Shin	**sh** (Shin is designated with a **dot at the upper right** of the character).
שׂ	Sin	**s** (Sin is designated with a **dot at the upper left** of the character).
ת	Taw, Tav	**t** or hard *'th'.*
ת	Thaw, Thav	Orig. pronounced like *th* in *thing.*

HEBREW VOWEL CHART

VOWEL	NAME	PRONUNCIATION
אָ	KAMATZ – קָמַץ	**AH** long vowel; as the *'a'* in *father.*
אָ	HATAF KAMATZ – חֲטַף קָמַץ	**AH** reduced long vowel; like *o* in *gone;* a schwa sound, with just a hint of the *aw* as in *saw.*
אַ	PATACH – פַּתַח	**AH, UH** short vowel sound; like *a* in *father* or *a* as in *was.*
אֲ	HATAF PATACH – חֲטַף פַּתַח	**AH, UH** reduced vowel; a *schwa* sound, with just a hint of the *e* as in *met.*
אֶ	SEGOL – סֶגּוֹל	**EH** short vowel; like the *e* as in *met.*
אֱ	HATAF SEGOL – חֲטַף סֶגּוֹל	**EH** reduced vowel; a *schwa* sound, with just a hint of the *e* as in *met.*
בְ	SHEVA – שְׁוָא	**EH** vowel or STOP; at the end of a syllable: silent; in middle of syllable: a *schwa* sound, *a* as in *alone.*
אִ	HIRIQ – חִירִיק	**EE** short vowel; *i* as in *machine.*

VOWEL	NAME	PRONUNCIATION
אִי	HIRIQ MALAY– חִירִיק מָלֵא	**EE** short vowel.
לֹ	CHOLAM CHASER– חֹלָם חָסֵר	**OH** long vowel; like the **o** in the word **alone.** The dot is to the upper left of the letter (with the Lamed, to the left of the upper stem, with other letters like the HET, it appears at the above left [חֹ]).
וֹ	CHOLAM MALAY– חֹלָם מָלֵא	**OH** long vowel.
וּ	SHURUK – שׁוּרוּק	**OO** long vowel; like **oo** in the word **moon.** The Shuruk is always [וּ] the Vav (right) with the dagesh (left).
אֻ	KUBUTZ – קֻבּוּץ	**OO** short vowel; like **oo** in the word **moon.** The Kubutz is the three dots, beginning under the left side of the Hebrew letter, and proceeding diagonally down to the right.
אֵ	TSERE – צֵרֵי	**AY** long vowel; like the **ey** in the word **they.**

Hebrew Cantillation

DISJUNCTIVES (separating) AND CONJUNCTIVES (joining)

"The Hebrew Bible is punctuated with an elaborate system of stylized inflections that delineate the most subtle nuances of meaning. For centuries this system was a purely oral tradition. Only the consonantal text was written down: the inflection had to be memorized. By the seventh century, the rabbis who considered themselves guardians of the sacred text became concerned that the correct melodic inflections were in danger of being forgotten. They therefore devised a set of symbols that would punctuate the text and indicate the proper motif to which each and every word was to be chanted. The *ta'amey ha-mikra* do more than merely indicate which syllable of each word is to be accented. For that function alone, one symbol would have been enough. not thirty. The *Te'amim* function as an elaborate punctuation system. a means of parsing the syntax of classical Hebrew. ..."

"On the page we could resolve the [accent] ambiguity if we had some form of detailed punctuation indicating which words are connected and which words are separated by a pause."

"The Masoretic system provides just such a system. There are two basic types of punctuation marks:"

• **"disjunctive accents,"** which indicate a pause or separation.
• **"conjunctive accents,"** which indicate a connection.[2]

---

[2]Joshua R. Jacobson, 'Chanting the Hebrew Bible', (Jewish Publication Society, Philadelphia, Copyright 2002), p23.

Five Levels Of Hebrew Cantillation

1) Level 1, known as the *Emperor Level.* Only two accents [cantillation marks] are in this category:

a) *Ethnacta,* with some exceptions, **expresses the logical end of the first half of a longer verse;** and

b) *Silluk,* **which is found in the last word of each and every verse in the Hebrew text of the Jewish Bible!**

2) Level 2, known as the *King Level.*
3) Level 3, known as the *Duke Level.*
4) Level 4, known as the *Count Level.*
5) Level 5, known as the *Servant Level.*

This introduction to Hebrew cantillation is very rudimentary. For a complete discussion I refer you to the book by Joshua Jacobson[3] or my web page devoted to Hebrew Letters, Vowels and Cantillation.[4]

In this chapter I started with a passage from Isaiah 55:6, *Seek ye Yehovah while He may be found.* I followed with a discussion on repentance, which is based upon having a relationship with Yehovah by returning to Him with humility. I discussed having a Scripture reading plan to help bring about a greater foundation to that relationship.

I began the end of the chapter with the iconic passage from Zephaniah 3:9 which speaks about turning peoples to a pure language (the Hebrew language being inferred).

Knowledge of the ancient Hebrew is critical in understanding the Hebrew text. Thus, I provided information introducing the Hebrew letters, followed by Hebrew vowels and cantillation.

---

[3]ibid
[4]My web page dealing with Hebrew Letters, Vowels and Cantillation is https://www.the-iconoclast.org/reference/HebrewLettersVowelsAccents.php

Epilogue

Last summer (2024), I felt driven to better understand Daniel 9, particularly the last several verses. I wanted to try to look at it again, but with fresh eyes, so to speak.

I was struck with the idea that the angel Gabriel seemed to focus on the city of Yerushalam and, within it, the most Holy place. Thus, I began to look at Gabriel's discourse differently at that time.

Continuing to review the text I noticed a natural break in verse 25, at "and for sixty-two weeks." To me, that separated the verse into two logical parts, each with an independent and complete expression of thought.

I decided to look at the Hebrew more thoroughly to see if it gave any clues. It was only then I thought to understand the greater purpose of the cantillation marks in the Masoretic text, as I only had a very basic understanding of them previously, being just concerned about verse endings with the **Sof–Pasuq** and **Silluq!**

To my own surprise, I learned about the **Ethnacta,** one of the two **Emperor Accents,** which separates longer verses into two sections. It so happened that the **Ethnacta** occurred in the word just before the word having the starting letter of a vav, which typically means, "and," in the translation for the phrase beginning with, וְשָׁבֻעִים שִׁשִּׁים וּשְׁנַיִם **"and for sixty–two weeks."**

Coming to this new understanding was almost devastating to me.

Like many others, for a long time I had understood that the essential messaging of the Messiah had been promulgated through popular books, like 'The Great Late Planet Earth.' Under that influence, I also had subscribed to the idea that the passages in Daniel referred to the coming of the person known as The Messiah.

My own world view was being transformed and I could not

continue in my former beliefs after understanding the *Ethnacta* cantillation mark as found in the end of the first part of Daniel 9:25 with the phrase עַד־מָשִׁיחַ נָגִיד שָׁבֻעִים שִׁבְעָה "unto **Mashiach nagid shall be seven weeks."**

Giving more thought to this new discovery, as I was again reading the text of Daniel 9, a revelation just came to me. I was meditating on what has transpired over the ages of time, and the sudden realization occurred to me, **that the angel Gabriel knew that his words would be misinterpreted to help justify a timeline for the coming of "The Messiah," and more specifically to Jesus of Nazareth!**

So, I started writing my thoughts down. I looked up references that I thought might add to a better understanding. I prayed about the writing, wanting to know if I should continue but also whether I should make the writing into a book which I would subsequently publish. This book is the result of that process.

Summary

In the introduction, I started with a presentation of how books like 'The Late Great Planet Earth' influenced modern society by bringing about Biblical Prophecy relating to the Messiah. The Christian premillennial/dispensational view, presented in that book, exposed the general populace to end–times views from a premillennial Christian perspective.

In the second chapter, *'Daniel 9:25,'* I presented two opposing interpretations of that prophetic text, first from a more orthodox Jewish point of view followed by a more traditional contemporary Christian view. I challenged both of those views.

Looking at the Hebrew text with its vowels and cantillation marks, I showed how the verse cannot be interpreted by associating " The Messiah" as coming at the end of the sixty–two weeks, but rather with the first part of the verse, which would have been 49 years after the word was given to return to and build Yerushalam.

In the third chapter, *'Ad Mashiach Nagid,'* I provided definitions for key words in the passage. I showed how that there is a possibility that the Holy city of Yerushalam may be considered to be **the conspicuous anointed"** (The Mashiach Nagid).

I also revisited Daniel's 62 weeks with a discussion of things that are known to have transpired at about that time, first with what may have been considered as desecrating the Temple Treasury, then the building of Herod's magnificent Temple. **I discussed why I believe that Herod's Temple was** <u>actually</u> **an** <u>abomination</u>!

In the fourth chapter, *'Gabriel Knew!,'* I explored the idea that the angel Gabriel was well aware that his prophetic discourse would be misinterpreted. No doubt, but both the Christian religion and subsequently the Islamic religion may have come about because of misinterpretations of the Hebrew text!

In spite of that possibility, **both the advent of Christianity and Islam have contributed to bringing about the knowledge of the One God to the world at large.** I believe that is profound! The result may be seen from the following passage in Habukkuk:

2 14 For the earth shall be filled with the knowledge of the glory of Yehovah, as the waters cover the sea. [Habakkuk 2:14 The Pill Tanakh]

In the fifth chapter, *'Biblical Judaism,'* I addressed the subject of just what is Biblical Judaism. I showed that **Karaite Judaism** is the better representation of what Biblical Judaism should be.

In looking at core principles, I presented views of the Ten Commandments from a Jewish viewpoint followed by a Roman Catholic view, giving comments on both.

In the sixth chapter, *'The Ten Commandments,'* I presented the Ten Commandments with verse snippets taken from the Leningrad Codex along with Hebrew font based forms and English translations. I provided an overview at the end of the chapter.

In the seventh chapter, *'Seek Yehovah,'* I discussed the idea of repentance as a basis for having a relationship with Yehovah by returning to Him with humility. Using the passage from Zephaniah 3:9, I discussed the idea of learning the Hebrew language, giving basic information as a start in that process.

Question: "What is the chief end of man?"

Answer: "Man's chief end is to glorify God, and to enjoy Him forever."

The Westminster Shorter Catechism begins by asking **"What is the chief end of man?"** The answer is **"Man's chief end is to glorify God, and to enjoy Him forever."**

That catechism goes on to expound upon ideas from the Christian New Testament, including giving references, mostly from the Christian Bible, for each expression of thought.

I agree that the chief end of man is to glorify יְהֹוָה Yehovah! What transpires after that, to me, is immaterial, because "It is not about me," **It's all about Him!**

There are many Psalms and other passages in the Jewish Scriptures which speak of such things. Psalms 25 has held a special place for me ever since I began reading Scripture on a regular basis at age 25!

תהלים כה:א‎-ג, ח‎-יג
Psalms 25:1-3, 8-13

כה א לְדָוִד אֵלֶיךָ יְהוָה נַפְשִׁי אֶשָּׂא:

25 1 [A Psalm] of David. Unto Thee, Yehovah, do I lift up my soul.

ב אֱלֹהַי בְּךָ בָטַחְתִּי אַל־אֵבוֹשָׁה אַל־יַעַלְצוּ אֹיְבַי לִי:

2 O my God, in Thee have I trusted, let me not be ashamed; let not mine enemies triumph over me.

ג גַּם כָּל־קֹוֶיךָ לֹא יֵבֹשׁוּ יֵבֹשׁוּ הַבּוֹגְדִים רֵיקָם:

3 Yea, none that wait for Thee shall be ashamed; they shall be ashamed that deal treacherously without cause.

ח טוֹב־וְיָשָׁר יְהוָה עַל־כֵּן יוֹרֶה חַטָּאִים בַּדָּרֶךְ:

8 Good and upright is Yehovah; therefore doth He instruct sinners in the way.

ט יַדְרֵךְ עֲנָוִים בַּמִּשְׁפָּט וִילַמֵּד עֲנָוִים דַּרְכּוֹ:

9 He guideth the humble in justice; and He teacheth the humble His way.

י כָּל־אָרְחוֹת יְהוָה חֶסֶד וֶאֱמֶת לְנֹצְרֵי בְרִיתוֹ וְעֵדֹתָיו:

10 All the paths of Yehovah are mercy and truth unto such as keep His covenant and His testimonies.

יא לְמַעַן־שִׁמְךָ יְהוָה וְסָלַחְתָּ לַעֲוֹנִי כִּי רַב־הוּא:

11 For Thy name's sake, Yehovah, pardon mine iniquity, for it is great.

יב מִי־זֶה הָאִישׁ יְרֵא יְהוָה יוֹרֶנּוּ בְּדֶרֶךְ יִבְחָר:

12 What man is he that feareth Yehovah?

Him will He instruct in the way that he should choose.

יג נַפְשׁוֹ בְּטוֹב תָּלִין וְזַרְעוֹ יִירַשׁ אָרֶץ׃

<u>13</u> His soul shall abide in prosperity; and his seed shall inherit the land.
[Psalms 25:1-3, 8-13 The Pill Tanakh]

My intention for writing this book, as well as my previous three[1], has been for the sole purpose **to glorify** יְהֹוָה **Yehovah!**

That is my chief hope! Moreover, I would certainly like to see many others have that desire, and that they would read the Hebrew–language based Jewish Scriptures, and its requisite translations, on a regular basis to help know יְהֹוָה Yehovah – the Almighty God – **with the purposes of glorifying Him!**

If this short book has helped to contribute to anyone glorifying יְהֹוָה Yehovah, that certainly is my own desire!

To that end, may this book help, even in a small way, **to bring about glory to** יְהֹוָה **Yehovah:**

ב יד כִּי תִּמָּלֵא הָאָרֶץ לָדַעַת
אֶת־כְּבוֹד יְהוָה כַּמַּיִם יְכַסּוּ
עַל־יָם׃

2 <u>14</u> For the earth shall be filled with the knowledge of the glory of Yehovah, as the waters cover the sea. [Habakkuk 2:14 The Pill Tanakh]

---

[1] My previous three books are as follows: 'The Real God Code: The Ten Commandments In The Leningrad Codex,' 'The Pill Tanakh: Hebrew–English Jewish Scriptures' and 'Jesus Cannot Be The Jewish Messiah*.'

www.ingramcontent.com/pod-product-compliance
Lightning Source LLC
Chambersburg PA
CBHW070759120626
46557CB00002B/664